HOW TO BE A GOOD MAN

A Standard and Timeless Guide

JUSTIN MEIER

Book Design by HMDpublishing

DEDICATION

To my son, Branden.

I pray you be the very best of men. I love you B.

CONTENTS

FORWARD BY CASEY DORLAND

My dad used to say, "If you aim at nothing, that's what you'll hit." He also used to say, "If you don't stand for something, you'll fall for everything." I know of no other time in our American history, when we have an entire generation of aimless, friendless and marginalized men. Men not just *aiming at nothing, but falling for everything.* Men apathetically buying into the marginalizing tide of our male culture. Men, who having grown weary of being unappreciated, have abdicated their roles as leaders and stabilizing forces in their home and in today's social construct.

I know my dad didn't make up the sayings I mentioned, but he never-the-less lived an intentional life. He often articulated simple truths like these, and encouraged a reliance on a real relationship with our Heavenly Father to guide daily decisions. Throughout dad's life, he made principled decisions dedicated to the God he knew and loved, and the wife and family he led. My dad was a real man. A *good* man.

Perhaps it's this picture in my mind of the *intentional* man my father was during his life, that makes the opportunity I've been given to write this forward such an honor. Author, Justin Meier, is the same kind of *intentional* man.

Justin was born and raised with humble beginnings and has been stretched in this life by injustice and circumstance. A man who learned through trial and error, personal adversity, and "aloneness" to trust God, and search out biblical principles and mentors to learn what it means to be an intentional man. Justin is a man of God, a man of honor, a man willing to aim for truth and speak it. A man with the courage to challenge and guide the next generation of men.

Justin takes on the tough topics, boys turning into men deal with. Topics others whisper about, or hide behind during locker room bravado, or most typically choose not to address at all.

Justin challenges boys to grow into more than marginalized men, he challenges them to be *good men!* Using conversational language, Justin provides needed tools for boys becoming men to lead a family, and to have a positive impact on their generation!

This is a book a father and son can read together. A book a mother can gift to her son with confidence that the message is grounded in biblical principles, relevant to the challenges their sons will face during this transition in their life.

Parents can use this book to help their sons unlock their potential and aim higher, be more than marginalized, and truly valued! Your son can be honorable, just, and true to the calling and potential intended by their creator. Justin encourages the next generation of men to be courageous and unashamed.

Justin's message to young men isn't just to try to keep them from falling for everything, rather, his message is that young men see the value they have as God's creation. It's their time to stand, not just as men, but *good Godly men!*

Justin is a man with feet of clay like the rest of us; however, he has dared to speak boldly to encourage boys longing to unlock their potential.

As a father myself, who had a *"good"* man as a role model for my life, I can't help but swell with fatherly pride as Justin speaks into our next generation of *good* men!

ACKNOWLEDGEMENTS:

First and foremost, I want to thank God for allowing all the pain he has in my life, for giving me correction, for giving me direction, for giving me purpose, and for providing me hope.

I want to thank my wife Michelle for all her support and encouragement. Her love, her good advice, her thoughtfulness, and the work she puts in to our relationship and family are valued beyond words. You are a precious gift and you make me a better man every day.

To my mom, I love you and I can't thank you enough for all of your prayers, encouragement, talks with me, and help you've given me over the years.

To my step-father, Dale, thank you for all the support from the moment you came in to my life. Thank you for all of your wisdom and direction you gave me. Thank you for doing your best to raise me right.

To my late father, Mark, I never met you but I have loved you since the moment I knew who you were. I wish I had you in my life, but I have hope I will meet you someday. Thank you for being such an inspiration for me in writing this book.

To someone who is like a spiritual father to me, Casey Dorland, who also helped edit this book and write the forward, thank you for your influence in my life. Thank you for your mentorship, your wisdom, your hope, and your help through some of the toughest times in my life... and being there to celebrate the victories. You have helped me become the imperfect but good, God-fearing man I am today.

To another father figure in my life, Daniel Hendrickson, I want to thank you for never giving up on me. I want to thank you for seeking truth and justice in all circumstances and for being an amazing grandfather. I want to thank you for serving our country so bravely, for serving your family so consistently, and for being an excellent model of leadership, strength, and masculinity. Your leadership has strengthened my character, my resolve, and who I am in total.

To my close friend and someone I consider a brother, Billy Grubbs, thank you for helping me get through what was one of the hardest times in my life, if not the hardest. Not only did you mentor me and counsel me through it, but you encouraged me to rise above it. You sacrificed your time, your effort, and even your finances to make sure I was headed in the right direction. You even encouraged me to write a book when I mentioned I was thinking about writing one, and now here it is! I can't thank you enough Billy, and as always… BOOOOOM!!

Finally, I would like to thank Diana Eilers for assisting with editing, Ken Darrow, M.A. who completed the final edits of this book, and Olayemi Bolaji for an outstanding book cover design. Without all of you, this book wouldn't be the final product it is.

INTRODUCTION

Every boy has a story.
Every man has one too.

Mine began in the 1980s, as a small boy in a small town, in northeast Washington.

Growing up I struggled with many things, as so many boys do. I struggled to find my identity, to find confidence, to fit in, to navigate my developing body and sexual desires, and to find my way and place in the world.

I remember feeling lost many times. I wanted answers to questions I didn't know how to ask, questions I was too afraid to ask, and questions that oftentimes I didn't even know I *should* ask. I wanted clear answers, a guide, someone or something to give me everything I needed. I wanted to feel secure, loved, and found. And by found, I mean *not lost.* And by *not lost,* I mean I wanted to know I was right where I was supposed to be, doing what I was supposed to be doing, and heading in a direction I was supposed to be going. But I grew up without many of those answers, and without those answers I *really* struggled as an adult, as a husband, and as a father.

The main things I struggled with as an adult were insecurity, confidence, and my sexual nature. I struggled to be a strong leader for my family. I struggled to behave like, and be, everything I should be as a man. But it wasn't until I reached the age of 31, during a time in which it felt like my life was falling apart, that I realized I had no clue what it meant to even "be a man." Shoot, I wasn't even sure if I could consider myself "a man" yet or if I was just a boy in a grown man's body! I thought, though, that if I knew what it meant to "be a man," and lived out what it meant to "be a man," maybe this would allow me to rebuild my life better than before. And maybe if I figured out how to "be a man" and shared that with other guys, I might prevent others from going through the same preventable struggles I went through in my life. Maybe I could help prevent them from experiencing the pain I went through in my life if they knew what I knew. So, I began to search for what it meant to "be a man." I searched for the answers to all the questions I had when I was a boy. I searched for the answers to the questions I *should have* had as a boy. I searched for the answers to the questions that would make me a man and lead to a good life.

During my search, though, I quickly realized it isn't enough to know how to "be a man." I realized that being a man (outside of the biological fact that a male has one X and one Y chromosome) is generally subjective in society, meaning many different things to many different people. And the lack of objectivity for what it means to be a man often leads to very destructive behavior.

What makes it even tougher when trying to figure out what it means to be a man, in today's day and age, is that masculinity is under attack like never before and is being pulled further and further into *more* subjectivity.

Boys grow up hearing things like man up, be a man, you can be a girl, be a *real* man, you can be whatever you choose to be, toughen up, traditional masculinity, toxic masculinity, real men should … (enter any stereotype about guys here). These are just some of the comments, messages, or labels most of us have heard at one point or another during our lives but don't have a clue what they really mean. Many are new messages that make things even more confusing for boys and cloud their sense of direction even further. All of these messages leave boys and men alike confused and lost, whether they realize it or not. Boys get bombarded with messages like these from an early age and many without a father or father figure to help understand them. Many boys grow up without someone who can help them define masculinity and provide a clear path toward becoming a man; someone who can teach them, guide them, and be a living example of what "being a man" means. Unfortunately, in many cases, fathers fail to teach and *live out* what it means to be a man. Even in cases where boys have good role models, a clear definition of masculinity can remain elusive.

But it is with the last sentence that we find a clue as to how to find the answers boys are looking for. With it, the conversation changes, with a clear purpose and direction. The clue is a key word. And that word is: *good.* And it is with this key word where the definition of masculinity, which is subjective, biased, a matter of personal belief or preference, changes to something objective, simple, and clear to understand. It is where my journey to find answers began to take shape and make sense. It is the word "good" that fundamentally changes what it means to be a man and what gives you, me, and this book meaningful purpose!

So, what is the purpose of this book? The purpose of this book is to clarify, define, and standardize what qualities, values, and characteristics it takes to be "a *good* man." Why it matters to be good and define good. To explore what good is, and what good men are, and why all guys should strive to become good men. To show it is *good* men females wish they shared relationships with and overall need men to be. To show it is good men society needs them to be but they have difficulty becoming.

As I elaborate on this subject throughout the book, I understand I may miss some topics or won't speak into your life the way you need, but I am certain there is enough information here to give you an excellent reference for how to be a good man and conduct your life as one. If nothing else, it will provide you with a great starting point.

I also hope this book will provide you with a simple resource to help teach your son(s) what it means to be a good man, or any boys over whom you have influence.

My goal is that you, or anyone who is exposed to the information in this book, will apply the characteristics outlined in this book to your life. And by doing so, you *will be* a much better man, bringing more stability, peace, and fulfillment to yourself and those around you.

Before I dive into the heart of the book, I want to note a few things. The first is that you will find references to the Bible in this book and the wisdom I've received from it. The reason I note this here is not to warn you but to challenge those of you who may not believe in the Bible. I want to challenge you not to immediately disregard what help this information may provide you just because it comes from a book you may disregard. I want to challenge you read what I, and it, has to offer you and simply see if it makes sense! Ask yourself, "If I do this, will it make my life better or worse, and will it have a positive impact on my family, friends, and others I interact with if I do it?"

The second note is it is okay to challenge the ideas I'm offering. See if there is another way, a better way. See if there is another way to create a definitive framework for what it means to be a good man. See if what I am proposing has the coherence and consistency to bring about goodness in life and in society. It is my hope that you will find what I am saying, and the source of much of it, the Bible, to be all of these things!

Lastly, in my professional life, I work with companies to *prevent* workplace injuries. To do this, I start by assessing the physical demands of a specific job. I look at all the individual tasks it takes to complete the job. Then I provide the company with a report outlining which tasks are most likely going to lead to an injury. This assessment provides the company with an *awareness* of the job's *areas* of risk. As part of this report, I recommend how to reduce high-risk tasks. My solutions create a standard for getting each job done safely, with less risk to the employee. I have approached this book in a similar manner. I assessed the previous and current state of what it means to be a man. I identified the problems in its current state, and this book is intended to provide realistic, standard solutions to reduce the many risks and negative effects of life associated with men not behaving like good men.

CHPT. 1:
WHAT IS GOOD?

What is a good man? Furthermore, what should a good man do? What should a good man say? What are the characteristics of a good man? What should a good man's values be? What moral standards should a good man follow to ensure he treats others well? Does a man even need to be good? And what does good mean anyway, and why is it important?

These are some of the major questions I sought to answer in my journey. To answer these questions, however, I first had to find a definition of what good is and means. And it couldn't be my own definition, otherwise mine would be just one more in a sea of endless definitions each person has.

Think about it; there are almost eight billion people on the planet as of this writing and that makes for a lot of room for individual interpretation as to what good means, right? For example, one person might believe physical violence is good, while another doesn't. What makes one person right and the other person wrong without a standard to reference? Why should I be trusted and not you? Isn't it just one person's ideas versus another's? To take it a step further, even if it were *groups* of people who agreed to a standard, what would make one group right and another group wrong?

You may ask, "Well, isn't it just common sense?" To that I would say what makes an idea or concept common? And even if we assume common means the majority, what makes the majority correct and the minority wrong? The bottom line is all humans are flawed and no human or human collective can or should be trusted to define good. It is too important of a standard to try to set ourselves.

So, **there must be a standard of good**, one that comes from outside of us, one that is coherent, consistent, and reliable in order to live good lives and allows us to have good relationships and good societies. But where do we find such a standard?

We find it in the Bible.

The Bible clearly defines good. It was given to humanity, by God, the moral law giver, who exists above and outside of humanity. The Bible makes clear what the standard of good is and always should be. It communicates all appropriate traits for what it means to be good. The Bible is our compass toward leading a good life, guiding us in the right direction. The Bible is also clear, consistent, and historically reliable. If you question its reliability, read the books *The Unshakeable Truth* by Josh and Sean McDowell or *Cold-Case Christianity* by J. Warner Wallace. They lay out the *abundance* of evidence that God is who he claims to be and the Bible is what it says it is.

Now, while the idea of using a Biblical standard of good will potentially turn many off and some may even mock the idea, try to stay with me.

Ask yourself, are there any other consistently valid definitions/models/resources for defining good that are not human? Are there any that maintain consistency and coherence in their truth claims? If there are, what makes them true?

You will find the Bible provides us with the best standard for good and, therefore, gives us the best resource to define what a good man is. It gives us our best shot at standardizing what a good man should be and how he should behave.

Even if you don't believe in God or the Bible, you can still apply the standards of good it gives us to your life. You can take them at face value, for what they are, and use them to improve your life here on Earth.

But know that if you stop and only use the standard of good the Bible provides you, to make this life better, you cannot replace something bigger, the saving of your soul. I want to encourage you to challenge the truth claims of the Bible and see if they are true. Not only for the purpose of the validity of everything in this book, but, more importantly, for your eternal self. You may be okay with not believing and that is your choice. I just want to make sure you know there is a difference and the possibility of so much more than improving this life alone.

Lastly, I want to present the Ten Commandments from the Bible as evidence of the Bible's standard for good. The Ten Commandments are a standard set of rules God gave humanity to *be* good. Rules that improve lives in one form or another. Rules that, at the very least, will prevent a lot of trouble in your life and the lives of your loved ones. Rules that were given by God, the creator of man, not man himself.

Try this exercise: I have listed the Ten Commandments below with a brief explanation of each. Read each statement, commandment, or rule and then ask yourself, if you applied each statement to your life, would your life get better or worse? Would you be behaving in a good way or bad? And if *everyone* followed these rules, would the world be a better or worse place?

1. I am the Lord your God who took you out of Egypt, out of the house of bondage.

God declares who *he* is and what *he* has done. He declares he is Lord and has freed the Israelite people from slavery. Here are some of the positive impacts this statement can have on our lives: By acknowledging there is a power greater than ourselves, we can admit we don't know it all; we can admit we will never know it all; we aren't even able to know it all. By acknowledging there is a power greater than ourselves, we can be humble. Humility that comes from understanding something is more powerful, wiser, and knowledgeable than *ourselves* helps us understand we *have more to learn.* And often, we have *a lot more to learn.* Understanding we are not perfect and no one can ever be helps us understand we all have room to grow.

When we acknowledge there is a perfect being who exists outside of us, it allows for the possibility to believe in the existence of objective goodness given by that being. We can value the necessity of a moral law giver, who defines goodness for us, rather than a subjective definition by us.

Finally, this statement is a reminder that we are free. That we *should* be free. Free from slavery and free from tyranny. Free from control by any higher power, *including* the God of the Bible. God may be who he is, but he allows us to choose between God or not. He allows us the freedom to choose between good and bad in every moment and live with the results. Either way, we are free to choose.

Freedom: *good*. Understanding we are not the center of the universe: also *good*.

2. You shall have no other gods before me.

"Gods" is a blanket term for *anything* other than the God of the Bible. Worshipping other gods leads to more emptiness in our lives rather than less. It usually leads to more bad behavior as well. What are other gods? Some are, of course, the gods at the head of some religions. But some are not what you might expect. These other gods can be trickier to spot and more detrimental to our lives. Some examples of these trickier gods are: money, sex, drugs, alcohol, fame, cars, video games, our spouses, our children, our houses, and our phones. The list goes on. None of these things can bring us complete fulfillment and relying on them is only going to bring disappointment because no amount of money is ever going to be enough. Our houses can always use an upgrade. Our spouses will never give us everything we want or need. Our children will disappoint us. And our kids need more from us than we could receive from them anyway.

So, by fulfilling this commandment, we are able to recognize the other gods in our lives and then release the expectations we have of them.

The other gods in our lives will *rarely* meet our expectations. And it is necessary to realize they will often be more heartbreaking than heart-making. If our focus is on these other "gods," we will find ourselves empty, frustrated, and discouraged.

Not consumed by possessions, relationships or material things: *good*.

3. Do not do evil in God's name.

Let's say you were to commit an act in direct opposition to a rule and you say the rule

giver told you to do it. If you do this, you ruin the credibility of the rule giver. This is what this commandment or statement is about. Here's an example. Let's assume you're a school principal and have a clear set of rules. The rules are clear about what you expect good behavior at school to be. Now let's say one of those rules is "do not punch people in the face." Additionally, everyone at school knows this is your most important rule. Now let's say you have a student whom you trust the most. They know all your rules and always follow them. All the people in the school know this child is your most trusted student. Now, let's say this student starts punching kids in the face. Not only that, he is punching people and saying you told him to do it. Unfortunately, you're unable to have a conversation and explain to the other kids what is going on. All you can do is leave your rule book out for people to read at their convenience. All you can do is hope they will continue to follow your rules and not listen to the kid punching everyone. This is what happens to God every time one of his believers breaks one of his commandments and does it in his name. And this is why this rule is so important. Because whether it's God or another authority figure, doing this undermines their credibility. And when we have undermined their credibility, how can they trust us?

Following good rules and not undermining our superiors: *good.*

4. Remember the sabbath.

The word sabbath means a time of rest. Biblically, the sabbath day first occurred on the seventh day, after God created the universe and Earth during the first six. On the seventh day, the Bible says God rested and blessed the seventh day and made it holy. He then commanded we "Remember the sabbath." This is important is because it marks a day to remember, to reflect, to rest, and worship God. Taking a day to rest and find gratitude can have many profound and positive impacts on our lives. Imagine putting our phones away, our computers away, and not turning on our TVs for a day. Imagine taking time to think, or not. Imagine spending quality time with our families at least one day a week or having quality time for ourselves. Imagine resting and letting the wonder of life fill us for at least a day. Imagine giving our minds the ability to enter a clear space where we can be grateful for all we have, create, plan, reflect, live and love.

A day of rest, reflection, relaxation and rejuvenation: *good*.

5. Honor your father and mother.

Many people have strained relationships with their parents, but honoring them is very important. I am not saying we need to accept abuse or control from them, but no matter the situation, we can acknowledge our parents made us. We can acknowledge our parents may have come from a troubled home themselves and they may have had strained relationships with their own parents. We can acknowledge our parents are likely treating us how their parents treated them. We can acknowledge that our parents have done the best they could with what they were and were not given. Again, this doesn't and shouldn't excuse abuse by a parent. Honoring good parents through thoughts and actions is easy, and having a healthy relationship with our parents is an obvious benefit, but how do we honor parents who have been destructive in our lives and caused us pain? We can honor them by releasing them from our negative feelings toward them. **We can forgive them.** It is important to release them and ourselves from the pain. It will give us the space to be a better person and better parent ourselves.

Acknowledging our parents did the best they could and releasing any ill will: *good*.

6. Do not murder.

Do not kill unjustly. Killing someone in self-defense, in a just war, or by accident, for example, is not murder. To kill is not always the same as murder and it is important to know the difference. Many times in history good men killed murderous, evil people to save innocent lives.

Not taking another person's life without just cause: *good*.

7. Do not commit adultery.

Many would agree the most important relationship in a person's life is the one with his or her spouse. No act undermines that relationship more than adultery. Or, to put it in a blunt way: sex with someone who isn't your spouse.

Not having sex or not committing our minds to having sex with someone who isn't our spouse: *good*.

8. Do not steal.

We can steal many things: property, money, innocence, love, time, and so on. Whatever we steal, we rob from another, oftentimes to a scale that is much worse than we ever could imagine. Stealing also damages another's trust in you. The more you steal the less you are trusted. The less you are trusted the less you are able to establish healthy relationships.

Not taking what does not belong to us: *good*.

9. Do not bear false witness.

Do not lie. Nearly all lies end up leading to immoral acts or evil behavior. Some of the worst lies have led to the greatest evils. For example, the Holocaust never would have happened had it not been for the lie told and believed that Jews were subhuman and needed to be exterminated. Lies that lead to evil are not good and should be avoided at all costs.

Not lying: *good*.

10. Do not covet.

To covet means to yearn, crave, or ache to take possession of something that is not ours and shouldn't be. When we covet, we can see ourselves having it, consuming it, or taking it. We can covet another person, another person's money, their car, house, family, or their happiness.

By *not* coveting we prevent the slippery slope leading to *acting* out in a bad or evil way. When we stop coveting, we find more fulfillment, which comes from the gratitude for what we already have.

Wanting certain things is okay. Desiring certain things is okay. Want and desire can be great drivers in life and can help you achieve goals, but it is important to know when we cross over into coveting. If you are not sure if you are coveting, ask yourself if what you want belongs to someone else. Ask yourself if you are feeling consumed by wanting it or wanting it *because* it belongs to someone else.

Not allowing our brains to want or take what isn't ours: *good*.

CHPT. 2:
WHAT IS A GOOD MAN?

A Good Man is:

1. A Rule Follower

I would be remiss if I did not begin by noting that a good man must follow the rules as I described in the previous section. These rules provide a foundation for what good *is* and, when followed, *should* lead to good behavior.

I will follow this section with a list of the characteristics all good men should have, but it's important that we build these characteristics upon a foundation of morals, or rules to live life by. Just as Jordan Peterson, Canadian clinical psychologist and psychology professor at the University of Toronto, has provided 12 rules for life in his international best-selling book

12 Rules for Life: An Antidote to Chaos, God has provided us his own 12, found in the Bible.

The first 10 I already mentioned in the previous chapter. The other two Jesus highlighted. These two are:

1. You shall love the lord your God with all your heart and with all your soul and with all your might.

2. You shall love your neighbor as yourself.

One might argue I could end this book right here, having given you the Bible's 12 rules for life, and tell you to follow them and that would be enough. But there is still much more to learn and talk about while unveiling how to be a good man. Having said that, the following are characteristics all good men should have. I describe what they mean and how you should use them in the sections that follow.

2. Independent

A good man is independent. This means you do not allow others to have control over your thoughts or your emotions, at least not in a way that could lead to bad behavior. This is true for strangers, family members (yes, even family members) or friends.

This also means you do not allow your own fulfillment and happiness to *depend* on others. You let go of everything you expect *of* and *from* them. At the same time, you hold yourself accountable for what you want and need in your life. You hold yourself accountable for what your family's wants and needs are as well.

You *must* do your best to control your *own* thoughts and opinions. Most importantly, you must control your own personal conduct because self-control is the root of independence.

When you control yourself, you don't expect others to take responsibility for *your* decisions, good or bad. You own who you are and what you do.

Your independence should also be continually strengthened by the standards you've chosen to live your life by. They should ground you and keep you steady.

In a nutshell, what you do and who you allow to influence your life should be completely up to you and 100% controlled by you.

Finally, a good man can show independence in a loving, thriving relationship by not *needing* a loving relationship. What I mean by this is if you are already filled with love yourself, and know your value, you don't *need* validation from another person. And in a love relationship, that attitude sets the other person free from expectations they *have* to make you feel good and feel loved. It alleviates a lot of unnecessary pressure on them and it sets you free to trust and give all you have to the person you are in a relationship with. So, make sure you are filling you without emptying them.

3. Wise

I define wisdom as: The moral application of knowledge resulting in improving one's life, their family's lives, and/or society.

As a good man, you take the knowledge you've gained and apply it to your life to live a more fulfilled, happier, and better life. And everyone who interacts with a good man ends up being a beneficiary as well.

The following is an example of the difference between knowledge and wisdom.

Let's say you learn how to drive and know all the traffic laws (*knowledge*). You decide to drive to work. You choose to leave for work a little early and follow the speed limits. You know this will increase your chances of getting where you need to go on time. You know leaving early will help prevent you from breaking traffic laws. You also know driving slower minimizes the risk of hurting anyone in the process (*wisdom)*.

You can also think of wisdom as "common sense." Common sense reveals itself by the obviousness of the decisions and actions we make. Decisions and actions that will most likely have good outcomes. Decisions and actions most people would agree are correct. It's when most people think about a potential solution to a problem and say, "Duh, that's what anyone should do in that situation. It's just common sense." There is an *obviousness* to the *goodness* of the action.

Wisdom is the *action* connecting knowledge to living a good life.

4. Honest

A good man is an honest man. A good man is truthful. And through your honesty, you prove yourself to be trustworthy. And everyone wants to have trustworthy people in their lives.

Honesty is also the foundation of integrity and all good men are men of integrity. They mean what they say and they say what they mean. More importantly, they *do* what they say.

Also, with honesty comes authenticity. Authenticity means you are who you are and you don't pretend to be someone or something you are *not*. Being authentic will reveal the *best* parts of who you are while exposing the *worst* parts of who you are. With both exposed, and a humble heart, you can shine a light on the good while working on improving the bad.

As an honest man, you know everything you say and do has ramifications for every aspect of your life and others. The people who know you see you are careful with the words coming out of your mouth. They see you are careful not to undermine or hurt those around you with lies. Having confidence in knowing what you say is true gives *other* people someone they can rely on and trust.

One last thought to chew on before moving on. I discussed the subjective nature of good when not relying on an external standard of good. Well, this is the same for truth.

Truth remains subjective by the definition you give it or by the definition anyone else gives it. Honesty and truthfulness must be from an external source.

One could argue that the definitive external standard for goodness and truth are one and the same. Either way, the point is this, if you are your only source of truth, then others are their only source for truth. And this creates accountability only for what you or they determine to be "lies." Where no external standard exists, how is your truth any different or more valid than theirs?

5. Faithful

Good men are faithful. Good men are loyal, consistent and steadfast. You and all those you know can count on you. You show up when you say you are going to show up. You do what you say you are going to do. You follow through on the promises you make and are thoughtful not to make commitments you may not be able to keep. Like honest men, faithful men "practice what they preach."

As it pertains to relationships, faithfulness means a few things. It, of course, means refraining from having sex with someone who is not your spouse. Faithfulness also means keeping your eyes, heart, and mind to yourself as you do your body. Good men keep all four areas committed and focused on their spouses. Eyes, heart, mind, and body. And it is through these acts of faithfulness that you affirm to yourself and your spouse they are the only one for you.

6. Loving

A whole other book could be written about the word love alone. I'm sure many have been written and are better than I could ever write. For the purposes of this book, I want to be clear and concise about one thing in particular; that the emotion of, or the term, love is often misunderstood and misused and it is important to understand the words and phrases we use, especially when it comes to love. Similar to how the phrase "be a man" is often misunderstood and misused, so is "I love you." Let me explain.

Love is often used to express a desire for something. You may say you love him, love her, love that car or love that house, but what you are more likely saying is you *desire* it. And desire leads to selfish ends. Oftentimes, we use the word love, confusing it for something less deep and meaningful, like desire. And it is very important not to confuse the two. Let me go deeper.

Loving is an action word. And *loving* a person would be better understood as *unselfish* desire. *Unselfish* desire brings *other* people fulfillment, pleasure and happiness. You want what is best for them, not always for you.

A good, *loving* man *unselfishly* desires everything good for those he says he loves. This is especially true for his family and he is willing to sacrifice what he must in order for them to live good lives. A good, *loving* man doesn't ask himself what he can *get* from those he says he loves. Instead, he asks himself, "What can I *do*, what can I *give*, or how can I *be* to show my true love?"

7. Kind

A good man is friendly, generous, and considerate.

This is another character trait that takes unselfishness. When you are unselfish, you are able to end your need for isolation, control of others, and greed. Unselfishness allows you to do things that fulfill the lives of others instead of always focusing on yourself. *Unselfish giving* is the root of kindness.

Try this mental exercise for a moment: think about what you are not *getting* in your life right now in whatever area(s) they may be (work, relationships, etc.). Now think about the person or persons you are expecting to fulfill these things for you. Now, forget what it is you are *expecting* from *them*. Instead, think about what the *other* person may *need* right now. Imagine you then do whatever you can to fulfill those needs instead of focusing on yourself. That's kindness.

Now, here is some clarification in regards to showing kindness. A good man may be kind, but it does not mean he must willingly accept abuse of himself or others. Many people who are abusive, destructive, and/or evil need to be handled carefully. Kindness may indeed be what these kinds of people need to change, but there must be intelligent decisions made to protect you or others from abuse while the abuser gets help. Simply put, understand that there are situations that require showing unselfish kindness, while others may require you to separate yourself from a bad or dangerous situation.

8. Merciful

A good man shows mercy. This is a tough one for some guys to hear, understand, and put into practice, so please pay close attention.

Good men *are* merciful. When you are merciful, you show compassion. You are able to forgive. With mercy, you show compassion and forgiveness even to those who may not be deserving. Instead of being vengeful, inconsiderate, and cold-hearted, you show empathy, concern and compassion. Instead of blaming the other person, you forgive them.

Through forgiveness and mercy, you release yourself from any mental or emotional prisons. You no longer remain bound by the chains of the situation or person(s) who wronged you. You can move on with your life.

The biggest hurdle to showing mercy and giving forgiveness is pride. Anytime you feel wronged and a reasonable solution isn't found, check your ego. See if your ego might be getting in the way of letting go of anger, hurt, or frustration. Work on your ability to fight your pride so you can be as forgiving, merciful, and compassionate as you can. This will not be easy and will be a daily struggle, but you and those around you will be much better for it.

As with kindness, there is an important balance to find with mercy. A balance between showing mercy without question and fighting for what is right.

You can fight for justice while releasing the injuring party of personal hurt at the same time. In some cases, it would be wise and right to do so. Finding an intelligent balance is key.

The take-home message is to make sure you let go of any mental or emotional control anyone may have over you. Do this by showing mercy, forgiving them of whatever wrong it was. You owe it to yourself to release yourself.

9. Gracious

A good man is gracious.

Think of this as giving your *undeserved* favor. Favor given without requiring anything in return.

For example, let's say you tell your son to clean his room before he can leave to go out with his friends. Before leaving, he assures you he has cleaned his room. While he is gone, you go into his room and find a couple pieces of clothing remaining on his floor. His desk is full of clutter as well. You can tell he did clean up some, but his room isn't as clean as you would like to see it.

You decide in the moment you are going to give him grace. Instead of criticizing him or telling him he must come home immediately until he does it "right," you let it go. You give him your undeserved favor and let it go. Providing him grace will increase relational growth (whether he realizes it or not) rather than creating a time of disagreement and relational division.

There are limits to a good man's grace, as there should be. Like I have noted, there are healthy limits to a good man's mercy and kindness. For example, a good man should not give favor to someone who is abusive or doing evil to you or others you know. The key is to *think* through each moment. Pick your battles with care and find a balance between fighting and giving grace.

10. Spiritual

A good man is able to enter and access mental space outside of his physical body. Doing this allows you to separate your physical body from your supernatural mind. Why is this important? Because it allows you to accept human existence is much bigger than the physical alone. It allows you the opportunity to think deeply, philosophically, and ponder big questions like, "Is there a God?", "If there is a God, which one is true?", "Are there such things as good and evil?", "Am I going to live my life by my own rules or by a higher standard?", "Where do we come from?", "What is the meaning of my life and life in general?", "What is my purpose?", and "When I die, will that be the end or is there more?" All of these questions can lead to a deeper life of fulfillment when answered.

I would like to provide you a personal example. It is through my belief in the God of the Bible that I have a sense of stability in my spirituality and mind. This stability brings greater stability to my physical body as a result. I rarely feel stressed, depressed, anxious, or fearful, even under the weight of some of life's greatest difficulties, many of which I will touch on later in this book.

I also have the perspective that my physical body is a gift and I do my best to take care of it as a result. Having the perspective that my body will die and a perfect life waits for me after death gives me peace.

My belief in the God of the Bible also gives me sound answers to many of the questions I posed earlier. My spirituality gives me greater access to humility, personal accountability, selflessness, and fulfillment. And through my belief in God, I am very aware that *I* am not the center of the universe.

If you are someone who is only connected to your physical body, then that is all you have to rely on. You only trust your life experiences and those of others. You will base life decisions and emotions off of what you gather with your five senses alone. And the result is often selfishness, bad behavior, and erratic emotions.

There is another, simpler advantage to acknowledging your mind, which is having an awareness of your mind. Many people live like robots, functioning to fulfill their most basic physical instincts. Once you become aware of your mind, you are able to access this space and explore it—and others. By connecting deeper and deeper with your own mind you begin to realize there is more and more to connect to. There is *a lot* more to understand. This is true of you *and* others. The more space you create to grow yourself the more space you create to grow with others. This will result in deeper and more meaningful relationships.

11. Present

No, I'm not talking about a *gift*, although a good man should *feel* like a gift to all those he interacts with and the lives he feeds into. But a gift is not the context in which I mean *present.*

What I am talking about is the ability to live not in the past or worrying about the future but live in the present.

For example, you may remember your past but when you are present in the moment, you do not dwell on it. Your brain may contain all the bad experiences you've had in the past, but when you are in the present, you don't think about them. Even in the present moments you *are aware of* them, but your wisdom allows you to think of how to learn and grow from them. This way, you can build yourself up, rather than break yourself down.

When you live life in the present, you don't dwell on the future. You *plan* for the future, of course. You set yourself up for future possibilities and successes, but you don't dwell or worry about what hasn't happened yet. You do not allow what hasn't happened yet to rob you of enjoying and experiencing this *present* moment. You don't *expect* anything from the future either. You are pleasantly surprised when good things are happening. But when bad things happen, you are wise enough to know they are inevitable and they will pass, so they do not affect you much.

Living in the present moment is one of the most difficult things I have done in my life. It is a daily and oftentimes moment-by-moment struggle. When you are successful practicing it, it can be one of the most rewarding experiences. For me, I remember more, enjoy life more, and feel more fulfilled. When I am able to ignore my past, not worry about my future, and live in and enjoy the moment, I *experience* life so much more. I experience it at a heightened level. A level far beyond the normal "I just want to get through this day" life. So, do your best to live *present* in each moment. You will be a better man for it.

12. Grateful

A grateful man is a happy man, and a happy man is a man who everyone likes to be around.

Think about the times in your life when you have felt ingratitude. Did you feel happier or less happy? Were you angry, frustrated, irritated? How do you think the people around you were affected by you when you were ungrateful? How did they feel when you were upset about not getting what you wanted instead of being grateful for what you had?

Think about the times in your life when you *were* grateful for something in your life. Did you feel more or less happy? Did you find your attitude was better or worse when you felt grateful?

If you haven't given much thought to what you are grateful for, try it. Make a list of the things you can be grateful for. These things can be as simple as being able to breathe, walk, or talk. Review the list often and add to it when new things come to mind. Make the effort to be aware of each of these things on a daily basis. Then self-reflect on your attitude. See if it is better or worse as a result of practicing gratitude.

When you are grateful for what you have, even for the smallest things, you will feel more fulfilled. You will feel happier. This is true even in the midst of the most difficult circumstances. Because even in the pain, gratitude can pull you out of despair, prevent depression, and keep you going. Of course, you will have to work harder to find things you can be grateful for during these times, but they are there. And finding them and being grateful for them can change the direction of your life!

I'm sure you've heard the phrase, "Gratitude will change your attitude." And this is so true! Think about how you will feel if you can live in the present moment while being grateful at the same time! Your happiness and sense of fulfillment *will* soar! So be present and be grateful. Be grateful and present. Practice it, and if you have to, fake it till you make it!

13. Pure

A good man can live a pure life by following the standard of good behavior. Remember, the standard I proposed were the Ten Commandments from the Bible. Purity can be best attained by following the last five Commandments specifically. They are do not murder, do not commit adultery, do not steal, do not bear false witness, and do not covet. A good man must fight his nature daily to practice good behavior, and it is good behavior that most often leads to good life outcomes and experiences.

This may be a tough idea to chew on for unbelievers of the Bible. If we are to have a standard of purity and good behavior, we must base it off one outside of ourselves and the Bible is the best we have. The better we are able to live by this standard the better we are for it, as well as those around us.

To understand purity another way, the more we stray from the standard of good the more *impure* we are. The more impure we are the worse our behavior is. The worse our behavior is the more we tend to lose those things that are good for our lives; things that bring lasting fulfillment, pleasure, and happiness.

The key is this; the purer we are the more chances we have to avoid self-inflicted destruction. The purer we are the more chances we have to avoid poisoning others with our bad behavior.

14. A Just, Passionate Fighter

A good man knows when to fight. Fight for what is good. Fight for your own well-being. Fight for your family or fight for others.

Fighting doesn't always have to involve physical force. Fighting can be a psychological or mental fight. Good men can use a variety of fighting tactics and methods. They can use any number of physical and mental elements to achieve victory over evil.

I realize I just finished describing the characteristics of a good man with "softer" terms. Terms like *kindness*, *loving*, *mercy*, and *graciousness*. But make no mistake, a good man knows when the scales have tipped and it's time to fight.

A good man is able to wisely *balance* when it is a time to fight and when it is a time to be kind. A good man should be able to balance between when it is time to fight and when it is time to extend mercy, grace and forgiveness.

Make no mistake, balancing these things is *not* an easy thing to do. You need to think through every situation first before deciding how and when to act. All while knowing sometimes you will need to act quickly. For example, as a parent you often extend grace to your children as they grow, learn, and explore the world. You realize they aren't perfect, they make mistakes, and failure is normal. However, there are times when your child crosses a moral line (let's say your child steals something) and you have to fight (discipline) your child to help them learn a life lesson.

So, what is the best way to determine when it is time to fight or not? First, you need to be aware that you *are* a fighter and you *can* fight and *will* fight if ever necessary. Second, if you are paralyzed in doubt about what to do, use every resource (people, books, articles) you can. Use them to help determine at what point you should lay down your arms versus when you should pick them up and fight; these same resources may be able to recommend the best tactics to engage in during a necessary fight too. Third, trust your instincts. If your gut tells you to fight, and it's a reasonable response in the circumstance, fight. Especially if you've had a chance to take a breath and your instincts continue to tell you to fight. When all else fails, trust your gut and respond.

If your health and safety are at risk if you do not fight, then you need to fight. If the health and safety of your family is at risk, you need to fight. These issues are clearer.

In general, as long as you do the *best* you can in some of the worst situations, you will have no regrets. See CHPT. 10: The Fighter for more information on this topic.

15. Confident

A good man is a confident man. Not arrogant, but confident. Confident in himself, confident in his desire to do good, and confident in what his purpose in life is. I believe the degree to which a good man has confidence correlates to the degree he has purpose.

Purpose in life makes up much of who you are. When you know who you are, you have more confidence. When you live your life with purpose, on purpose, confidence elevates you, oftentimes to a level you didn't know you were even capable of. It is as if you don't have a choice but to be confident because you are driven by your desire to fulfill your purpose. Nothing else seems to bring you down, scare you, or get in your way.

What if you find you are *not* confident as you work towards your purpose? If that's the case, you should rethink your purpose. Ask yourself, does your purpose excite you, drive you, or ignite you? Is working toward your purpose fulfilling? If not, and you have been at it a while, rethink your purpose. There is nothing wrong with doing that. It's okay if this takes a little time. You will find it and you will know when you find it because everything in you will come alive and your confidence will surge.

Here are some other questions to ask yourself. How many guys do you think, without hesitating, can state their purpose in life when asked? Can you state yours? How many guys, including yourself, do you think have a clear purpose and sense of meaning in their lives? Further, if any of these guys *do* have a purpose, how many of them would produce good as opposed to fulfilling selfish desires only? For example, how many men find purpose in helping others? How many men find purpose in fighting injustice or being a committed husband and father? Do most men believe their purpose is to make as much money as they can or to "live their best life" (whatever that means)? Or is their purpose to sleep with as many women as possible, or have as much fun as possible, or to "just do me," etc.?

The key here is to make sure you find a purpose that will produce good. Because if you do, your confidence *will* soar!

16. Humble

A good man is humble.

Humility begins when your sense of being perfect ends. When you are humble, you realize you *always* have more to *learn* and have more to *give*. Being humble does not mean you can't still be confident. It just means you need to balance confidence with humility while leaning on the side of humility. Think of it as having *quiet* confidence. You are confident, but you are quiet about it.

There are times when you should assert your known abilities to get a job done. Jobs that otherwise wouldn't get done or get done as well as they could if you did not apply your skill set to them. But you have to have a good sense of your own abilities and know how to use them. On the other hand, you may *not* be completely aware of your strengths or weaknesses and need to find these out. Regardless, even if you do know your greatest strengths, just because you may excel at something doesn't mean you have to brag about it. It doesn't mean you always need to make sure you insert yourself into every situation, especially when someone else could grow or learn from the same opportunity. The key is to find a way to balance between talking about and/or using your gifts and talents and knowing when to keep quiet.

Humility doesn't mean you should stop learning or growing either. Keep growing your gifts and talents and use them to the absolute best of your ability. Use them in the most efficient way possible. Maintain constant self-awareness and situational awareness so you can use them best. Doing this will make you a better employee, a better boss, a better father, a better husband, a better son, a better friend, and a better human being.

17. Responsible

A good man is responsible. And with responsibility comes greater accountability, dependability, reliability and trustworthiness. To be responsible, you must first acknowledge all the things you are responsible for.

So how do you identify the things you are responsible for? Start by identifying the things you find valuable. Even the things you *should* find value in but aren't so obvious. All the things you should protect, nurture, and care for.

Take your job or your belongings, for example, or your relationships and character. These are all things you are responsible for.

Make a list of all these things. They can be physical things like people, money, a home, or a car. They can be intangible things like character, good behavior, and personal development. Once you have the list of things you find valuable, you will have the list of things *you* are responsible for. This list may even have some similarities with your list of things you are grateful for.

Knowing what you are responsible for will help you see what you should be taking more seriously in your life. Things you should be prioritizing, caring more for, growing and feeding in a positive way.

By being responsible you build and grow everything in and around you that's important.

CHPT. 3:
YOU'RE *NOT* GOOD ENOUGH

Many of my struggles began after an incident that occurred early in my life. Something that rocked my world and broke my heart.

I was about eight years old and my stepfather was driving us back home from a trip to Spokane, Washington. I loved going places with him and this was one of the few but memorable trips he and I took during my childhood. This trip was about to stand out from the rest, but, unfortunately, not in a good way.

I remember my eyes darting back and forth between my stepfather and the window. I remember watching the land-scape flashing past us as he told me he was *not* my biological father. I remember him telling me when I was just a newborn, my biological father left me and my mom. I remember him telling me how, a short time later, my biological father gave me up for adoption once he realized how much money he would save in child support. I remember my stepfather telling me he adopted me and he was now my dad.

It was like being told to drink every drop of water sprayed into my mouth from a fire hose but there was nothing I could do to consume it all. I was doing my best to take it all in so I could somehow understand.

After I heard all the information, I remember acting as if everything was okay. On the outside I pretended I was fine and it all made perfect sense. I acted like I put it all behind me right then and there. But on the inside, I felt confused, heartbroken, and abandoned. And it was on my mind every day after.

I felt abandoned by my father. I felt as though he abandoned me for another life including a woman other than my mom. I felt abandoned for a life where he prioritized saving his money over saving his family. I was left feeling like my father had no desire to see his son, a human he helped create.

I didn't realize it at the time, but I may as well have had "JUSTIN MEIER: NOT GOOD ENOUGH" tattooed on my forehead that day. My sense of value was confused. My sense of identity had been shaken. I felt lost. There was so much I wanted to understand but didn't.

A deep sense of shame, anger, resentment, sadness, and heartache began to grow in me. I decided that day I would move forward with my life. I decided right then, right in that painful moment, I was going to *heal* me by *hurting* him. I was going to make my biological dad regret the day he left me and my mom. I was going to prove to him and myself that I *was* good enough.

You see, my stepfather also told me that, if I wanted to, when I turned 18, he would take me to visit my biological father. And boy was I going to do just that. I set out to be the best and most successful kid possible. I was going to throw every one of my successes right in my biological father's face someday. I was going to make him regret he was never a part of them. I was going to show him, in as many ways as I could, that I *was* good enough.

Flash forward to September 2000. I was only eight months away from my 18th birthday. I was going into my senior year of high school and was on track to do exactly what I had set out to do. By the time I would meet my father, I would be the scholar athlete of the year for the entire Great Northern League. I would be an honors student holding a near 4.0 GPA. I would break four school records in track and field and win a state championship in the long jump. And, by all external standards, I was a good Christian boy with good character. I was more than ready and, for all intents and purposes, armed to the teeth to show him just how *good enough* I was. But life stepped in, slapped me upside the head and crushed my heart one more time.

On the morning of September 3, 2000, my stepfather woke me up and handed me the Spokane newspaper. In it, I read my biological father's name and saw his picture next to it. This was the first time I had ever seen a picture of him. I proceeded to read a short summary explaining how he died in a car accident the night before.

I was crushed. The hole in my life would now remain empty forever. The hole I had once hoped to fill with my father's regret and acknowledgement of my value would remain. In fact, the hole felt wider and deeper than ever.

To add salt to what seemed like a painful enough wound already, I decided to attend his funeral. There, I heard his voice for the first time, but he wasn't speaking, he was *singing*.

I found out that day he was a recording artist and had an incredible voice. Some of the songs he recorded, songs he had intended to sing at his own father's funeral, were now being played at his own. As I sat near the back of the church sobbing; I listened to my father sing, breaking me in the moment. I was devastated. For a moment, I felt completely lost. The voice I was listening to sing I would never hear say, "I'm sorry," or, "I love you," "I care about you," or, "You *are* good enough."

The loss of my father and the void he left in me led me to make another life choice. From that moment on, I decided if I ever had the chance to be a father, I would never crush my son like my dad crushed me. I would never abandon him like my dad abandoned me. I was going to be a *good* dad. And I was going to ensure my kid(s) never felt like they weren't good enough.

You're Not Good Enough

So this is the part where I am supposed to tell you, "You are good enough," or tell you, "You are perfect just the way you are," right? This is the part where I tell you to always make sure your kids feel like they are good enough, right? I am supposed to tell you I have spent all my time as a father making sure my kids never feel like they aren't good enough. I am supposed to tell you no matter what the world says, or what anyone may do, you *are* good enough.

Well … you are wrong.

That is not what I am going to tell you because it is not true, because you're *not* good enough.

I am not good enough. My kids are not good enough. No one is good enough. Because no one is perfect. Anyone anywhere can always do and be better.

Good men need to know and teach others the difference between *personal value* and whether or not someone is "good enough." They are two different things because personal value or worth has nothing to do with someone being "good enough" or not. And confusing personal value with the concept of being good enough leads to many poor character traits and behaviors in men.

First, not being good enough does not mean you do not have value. It just means you are human and make mistakes!

Second, personal value is unchanging. It is equal and inherent for all human beings and no one can take your value away from you unless you allow them to. More on that soon.

Third, if you do not feel good enough it is because of one of two things. Either it is because you are in fact not good enough or you are confusing it with a loss of personal value. The key is to make sure you never lose your sense of value while maintaining a humble sense of your own imperfection, allowing for the space to grow personally. Make sense? If not, let me explain further.

If you believe you *are* valuable, no matter what other people say or do, no personal attacks will affect you (past or present). And if you can understand you are not good enough, you can improve as a person!

For example, we all may have equal and inherent value, but you and I can always be better at any number of things, none of which affects our personal value as a human being. You and I can be a better listener, a better talker, a better son, a better father, a better student, a better teacher. Name almost anything and you and I can be better at it. But not being good enough is often not the cause of the pain in our hearts. It is a sense that our personal value is being attacked and reduced.

Think about it. Doesn't "I am worthless" strike more at the heart of what is going on inside of us versus *feeling* good enough or not? Doesn't lack of self-worth explain much better what is going on inside us emotionally? It is certainly what was going on inside of me when I felt abandoned by my father. But feeling like I wasn't good enough had nothing to do with my personal value as a little kid! There is not one thing I could have been better at then or now that would have brought my father back, right? There is not one thing I could have been better at that would have made him not leave, right? But him leaving was what left me feeling like I wasn't good enough, when in reality I was feeling worthless. I wish someone would have made the point to show me the difference between these two ideas as I grew up so I wouldn't confuse them. If someone had, I am certain I would have been a much more secure man much earlier in my life. I would have been secure in my value as a person, knowing it is unchangeable, no matter how others treated me. I would have also come to the realization that I will always be flawed and can improve myself while not being worried about trying to turn myself into something I am not, just to prove my worth to someone else so *someone else* might find me valuable in their eyes.

How many situations have happened like this in your life, which have been out of your control? How many people have you wanted to find value in you but they either didn't or were not good at showing it? Everything you value, and I mean *everything,* in this world will let you down at some point. Everything has the potential to extract value from you if you let it. Everything and everyone you value will likely disappoint you, hurt you, and leave you feeling like you have little or no value at one time or another. It sucks, but it's true, and many of you have likely already experienced this.

Even your purpose (assuming you believe you have one) will leave you feeling worthless at times. The times when it seems like you aren't fulfilling your purpose. The times you fall short of your goals. The times when the most important people in your life question your purpose and your motives.

Even your parents can make you feel worthless at times. Even your spouse, your kids, your friends and, yes, even your religion can make you feel worthless at times.

The key to changing this is to *understand and believe* what your personal value is. You must always remember your inherent value, not what others think of you; it will make you a more confident man.

To illustrate this concept, let's use the example of a verbal fight.

Verbal fights are often made worse by assuming the person criticizing us is attacking our value. This is true for fights between parents and kids, husbands and wives, co-workers and friends. But how many of the people we fight with are actually trying to attack our value? More often than not, they are just pointing out an area of ourselves that, in fact, could be better. While many fights may devolve into deliberate personal attacks, most don't start out that way. Rather than having a sense of lost personal value in these moments, we should work to set value aside completely. We need to know in all situations we are valuable no matter what. It is not given by the other person and cannot be taken by them. Then, with your sense of value secure, you can take time to explore what ways you are not good enough, how you can be better. You can let your guard down and be a humble learner.

Every life situation will be different. Every sense of personal attack will be varied, but it is key to ask yourself with each attack, *Can I do anything to improve?* Is what the other person is saying, no matter how harsh, true? If it is true, make the change. If it is not true, let it go. Don't hold on to the bad feeling. When it seems as though others are trying to break you down in life, you can choose to *build up* or *break down*. The choice is up to you alone. Do your best to find a balance and learn how to differentiate between attacks on your value and the areas in which you are weak. Learn how to move forward with your life in a positive manner either way.

You Are Valuable

Before moving on to the next chapter, I want to do an important deeper dive into personal value because questions may still remain for some of you, like: Where does my value come from if not myself or others? How do I *know* I am valuable? I have natural, inherent value, and why does it even matter?

Start by asking yourself, does personal value come from things within this physical world alone? If does, doesn't your sense of value fluctuate up and down dramatically, depending on how fulfilling each thing or experience is? Ask yourself, does your sense of value come from within you? If it does, doesn't your sense of personal value fluctuate up and down dramatically depending on how you are feeling at any given point? And doesn't each of these sources have subjective value, likely to leave you feeling less valuable rather than more?

So, what is the answer?

The true answer is a lot like the answer to what is good, where it comes from, and why it matters.

The answer is; not only are you valuable as a human being, but your value is definable, unchangeable, and understandable. Your value is greater than you could ever imagine too and *must* come from a source from outside of you. Otherwise, you are a clump of matter who gets your value based on your own changing internal feelings or the opinions of anyone else. You would serve no purpose. You could use others however you saw fit, and be used by others however they saw fit, without consequence. Because, after all, if you have no value, who is to say you, or they, can't be treated poorly?

Ultimately, who is to say one person has value, a certain level of value, or no value at all?

Personal value must then, just like the definition of Good, originate from the Bible and the God of it because there is verse after verse in the Bible describing the *immeasurable* value God has gifted us with. For everyone equally. Value that is unchangeable. Value that is unaffected by anything or anyone in this world. The God of the Bible numbers the hairs on your head (Luke 12:7). He knew you and cared for you before you were born (Psalm 139: 13–16). He sent his perfect and blameless son, Jesus, to die for all your wrongdoings so you wouldn't have to, if you simply believe in him (John 3:16). And those are only a few of the many examples of his value for you. His value for you is perfect, and it is rooted in a perfect, good God who exists outside everyone. Nothing can change it.

I know this will read as ridiculous to many people, but I wouldn't mention it if I hadn't lived it, experienced it myself, and believed it to be true. Believing in the care and value God has for each person is a most fulfilling sensation. It is an internal fulfillment very difficult to diminish, especially the more his value for you is understood, a value better than any sense of self-worth that could ever be given to you by this world or yourself, both of which are senses and sources of self-worth that will take from you more often than they give.

In summary, no, you are not good enough. You are human; an imperfect being, but you have inherent, equal and immeasurable value. And when you begin to understand your value, you can more easily let the pain and disappointment that comes from this world and the other imperfect beings in it go. And after you let go, with two open hands, reach out and grab a better future. This is an essential understanding to becoming a good man. One who can let go of past, present, and future hurts. One who can let go of his pride, be secure in his value, and open himself up to criticism so he can improve.

CHPT. 4:

HOW TO BE A GOOD DAD

One night in January 2015, the trajectory of my ability to be a good father changed forever.

By this time in my life, I had already enjoyed six years with our strong, beautiful daughter and three with our tenderhearted son. But as I was nearing a divorce, after a near 10-year marriage, the night came when our kids' new reality would begin. A reality that would open their eyes to the fact that a true division had taken place between their mom and their dad. A realization that things would never be the same for them again. This evening would be the first they would sleep in beds that had not consistently been their own. And for those who know about divorces involving children, know about the "parenting plan," ours was about to begin.

When I dropped the kids off for the first time that evening, my daughter seemed to take the change in stride. She entered the house I was dropping the kids off at without trouble. But my son, well, he was quite different. After my daughter entered the home, my son remained with me in the open doorway, grabbed hold of me, and began to cry.

As we stood there facing each other, his head between my legs, I told him he needed to go and he reached up for me. I picked him up and once in my arms he hugged my neck so tight and he started to sob. His sobbing escalated as I tried explaining to him why he had to let go. I tried to help his mind come to grips with why he had to walk away and leave everything that was once normal behind him. But, no matter how many words I used, and no matter how many different ways I tried to use them, there was no convincing him everything was going to be okay. It was as if in this moment, his little brain had truly grasped the reality and finality of the division between his parents and what it meant for his life.

We held on to each other longer and I didn't want to let go of him, but it was getting further and further past the time for him to go. So, I finally, reluctantly, began peeling his little arms away from my neck. But the more I pulled the harder he squeezed. Once I managed to free him from my neck, I took him and set him down inside the doorway we had been standing in for who knows how long and firmly turned him around so he couldn't latch on to me again. As soon as I set him down, he immediately tried to turn back toward me, but I wouldn't let him. I held him facing away from me.

With his back now turned to me, realizing he was fighting a losing fight, he started to cry even harder. And that is when I forcefully pushed him away from me. I pushed him in through the open doorway, telling him he had to go. But he didn't move from his new position. He just dropped his head low and continued to sob.

As he stood there, just a step or two inside the doorway, I told him again, but more forcefully this time, that he *had* to go. And as badly as I wanted to cry myself, drop to my knees, hug him and tell him everything was going to be okay, I held my place and held back the tears. I knew I had to keep it together.

Finally, after what seemed like forever, but was likely just seconds, he found the strength to take his first step away from me and started walking up the staircase directly in front of him. I watched as he labored up the stairs weeping, head down, looking completely dejected. Utterly defeated. And once he reached the top of the stairs he didn't look back, he just kept walking. He turned the corner to his left and disappeared. I then turned myself and started to walked away. My heart lodged deep in my throat and it wasn't until I entered my empty house and was alone that *my* new reality set in. My marriage was over, my kids were gone, and I was alone. And it was in this heartbroken, lonely, tear-filled moment that I hit rock bottom.

Everything I had set out to do as a dad fell apart. I felt like a complete failure. My family unit was forever fractured. I wouldn't be able to be there for my kids like I had hoped or be with them every day as they grew. I had a deep sense that I had abandoned them, failed them, crushed them, and broken their hearts.

It is this experience that made me look at my life, determine who I was as a man and father and who I was going to be from that day on. It forced me to look at what I stood for, what I would stand for, and what I believed in. I began a journey to find the answers to these questions about my life and about my faith. It was this experience that led me to ultimately find out what it meant to be a man, a *good* man, a good dad, and a good husband. And it has been my hope ever since to share my stories and insights in hopes to prevent even one other boy, one other man, or one other family from going through what we've gone through.

How to Be a Good Dad

Show up.

That's it. Show up. It's the simplest and best place to start. Every day you can be with your children, in as many moments as you can, show up. Show up with the best *you* that you can muster. Show up physically and show up mentally. Let go of the past, forget about the future, and just live in this moment with your kid(s). Forget about what you *want* in these moments and realize *you* are what your kids *need* in these moments. It won't be perfect. It won't be pretty at times, but you will be there. And if you look in the mirror, you may see this is the same thing you needed from your own dad.

To understand the impact on children when fathers *don't* show up, here are some important and sad facts.

Children who grow up in fatherless homes are:

1. 7 times more likely to become pregnant as a teen.
2. 4 times more likely to live in poverty.
3. 2 times more likely to drop out of school.
4. More likely to commit crimes and be imprisoned.
5. More likely to suffer from obesity and abuse drugs and alcohol.[1]

According to a report from the U.S. Department of Justice, "What Can the Federal Government do to Decrease Crime and Revitalize Communities?", children from fatherless homes account for:

1. 63% of youth **suicides.**
2. 90% of all **homeless** and **runaway** children.
3. 85% of all children who exhibit **behavioral disorders.**
4. 71% of all **high school dropouts.**
5. 70% of **juveniles in state-operated institutions.**
6. 75% of **adolescent patients in substance abuse centers.**
7. 75% of **rapists** motivated by displaced anger.

Fathers are important and being an impactful one starts by *showing up*.

Learn from the mistakes of those who've suffered before you so you don't make the same.

To be a good dad, you *must* find sufficient motivation to change. And you should find plenty by looking at the history of the fathers who failed before you. Fathers who left a legacy of hurt and pain. Mistakes by fathers who left a road map of where *not* to go. Maybe one left by your own father.

Having said that, if you are a perfect dad and don't need to change, then this part isn't for you. But for everyone else, I guarantee there is at least one aspect of your fathering that can be improved. In order for you to be the dad you need to be and *should be*, one area must be removed or improved; one area in which you can do better than your father and fathers before you.

But most guys don't like change. And guys certainly don't like to admit we are wrong or, God forbid, have flaws. We struggle deeply with humility and the ability to self-reflect. We struggle to see who we really are and what we should change. But we often can't and won't change until we find incentive enough to do so. So, whether it be one of my experiences I have shared or will share or someone else's, use it as fuel to change. Maybe even take the time to imagine some of your own worst-case scenario nightmares in order to make a change. Scenarios where your family's life falls apart as a result of your poor decisions. Take the time and find the motivation. *Whatever it takes, do it!* You, your children and the generations to follow are worth it!

Awareness is the key to change.

Speaking of humility and self-reflection, it is important to realize you don't know what you don't know. What do I mean by this? I mean if you don't know a problem exists, you can't fix it. If you don't know where your blind spots are, you can't see hazardous areas to avoid.

Becoming aware applies to all areas of being a good man, but especially when trying to be a good dad. So, here's how to pinpoint, and become aware of, your weak spots:

First, humble yourself. For those of you who don't know what humility is exactly, look it up, study it, and practice it. If you don't, you waste you and your family's time acting as though you genuinely care to change. And you miss a key component to *authentic* change.

Second, self-reflect. Search your past and your present. Analyze what influences have affected you positively *and negatively* and learn from both. Keep the good; learn from and erase the bad. Also, think deeply about your character traits. Use our "standards of a good man" list of characteristics and go through each. Take note of the characteristics with which you need work.

Third, ask others for input. Start by asking your significant other what they think you can do better. Let your guard down and humbly listen to their input. Expect them to say the worst, allow them the freedom to do so, and take notes about the things they say.

If they give you all positive feedback, they are probably lying to you. If they are honest, you will probably have a fair list of things to work on. And if any of them hurt, these are probably the ones you should start with. And even if they do hurt, say thank you, don't get angry, and get to work.

It is worth repeating that the areas you need to work on the most will be the ones you're offended by and want to deny the most. Reflect on them. Study them. And use any sense of criticism as fuel to get better and refine yourself.

Then ask trusted family members or close friends what you can do to be a better father. Ideally, they will tell you the brutal truth about what you can do better as a father. Make sure you provide them with total freedom to communicate any and every criticism. Then digest the information as you did before and get better. Do better.

Pick your battles.

One of the greatest lessons I've learned when raising my kids is the need to pick my battles. Doing this has made me a better and more relaxed father. I know it has made my kids better and more relaxed kids.

There was an earlier time in my life when I felt my kids' *every* move and act was under direct scrutiny. Once I began to picking my battles carefully, I could see their spirits lift. I could see our relationships improve and trust in one another grow.

Picking your battles isn't easy though. It is difficult to know what is worth fighting for and what isn't. It is a constant struggle within you and what is going on around you and with your kids. It's a constant fight in your mind deciding where you should put your foot down and where you shouldn't.

How *do* you decide where to put your foot down? Start by focusing on issues that directly relate to your kids' character and safety. Issues that will influence most *who* your kids will become, not issues that influence how well they will clean up their messes. Issues that will keep them alive and thriving instead of issues you know you could easily let go.

Stay *away* from the minor issues. Stay away from making major things out of minor things. This will help you avoid alienating and frustrating your kids. They will feel less like you are trying to control every single thing they say and do. They will feel like you are focused on shaping them in ways you rightfully should be.

But what about things that come up quickly and unexpectedly? Battles you haven't had a chance to think over yet? To address these, get in the habit of doing a quick assessment in your mind. For me, I stick to character and moral development. Typically, I quickly ask myself, "If I don't address this, are my kids going to treat others better or worse?" because the battles that affect how my kids treat others are usually the "hills" I am willing to die on. Treating other people how you would like to be treated is something I expect my kids to live out. And this is something most parents are unified in teaching their kids too.

To give an example, if one of my kids were to steal a toy from another child, then I am going to make my child give it back. I will have them apologize and, if old enough, ask my kid if they would like it if another kid stole *their* toy. But if at dinner my kid doesn't eat all of the food on their plate, I'm going to let that slide. If I hear my kids arguing, and neither is assaulting the other's character, I will let them figure it out. If one of my kids picks out clothes to wear I wouldn't have, but they look presentable, I'm keeping my mouth shut.

In each situation, I try to remember my ultimate goal is to help my kids become good people, not micromanage them. And building up, not breaking down, my relationship with them is key to doing that.

You cannot lead an alienated heart and expect it to follow, let alone pass on the values you hope to instill in this and future generations.

So, when your kids see the consistency of the battles you are willing to fight—ones that relate to them becoming good people—it is easier for them to accept and understand what is important. When you fight over character building, rather than fighting over every little thing, you don't leave your kids wondering about what is important.

No matter how tough parenting gets, accept you won't have all the answers, and NEVER GIVE UP.

I remember a time when I felt pretty good about my parenting. Really good, actually. Even though my kids were going through a lot of turmoil in their lives, I felt like my parenting was what was keeping them on a good path. Raising them, for a long time, felt pretty easy. But for my son, that all changed during a period of time when he was about nine. For whatever reason(s)—and trust me I tried to figure out every possible reason I could (but failed)—he became really hard to deal with. His attitude was terrible, he started being really mean to other people, he would back-talk constantly, and the smallest correction I tried to give him would turn into a huge fight and the end of the world was upon him. It seemed like he was in trouble all the time and the sweet, tenderhearted boy I knew and loved was gone! I tried everything to figure out what was causing his change and help him through it, but nothing worked. I tried long talks; I tried short talks; I tried no talks. I tried taking items he cared about away; I tried taking screen time away; I tried taking time with his friends away. I tried and I tried and I tried and nothing worked. And that's it. Nothing worked. Period. Eventually, he did grow out of his bad attitude and returned to be more like the sweet kid he had always been, but not because of anything I did.

When I reflect back on that time, what I learned from that phase my son was going through is that we don't have all the answers as parents sometimes. Sometimes we have to accept the fact that our kids are going through some things and acting out in ways we may not understand or ever understand. And as hard as it is to accept, accepting that this is actually normal for kids to go through is okay.

Accepting this doesn't mean you should excuse the behavior or give up. It just gives you the space let go of the stress, anger, and frustration your kid's behaviors might be causing you and realize all you can do is the best you can in each day and in each situation!

As parents, during difficult times, you may need to just be consistent in your discipline, consistent in your teaching of values, consistent in your desire to see your kids win (without sacrificing their character growth), stay present, and let the outcome be what it will be. Ultimately, your kids are going to be who *they* will be, not who you *want* them to be. They will grow into adults and will make all their own decisions. And all of *their* decisions will cause consequences in *their* lives, good or bad. Knowing how to balance what to let go of, when to let go, and how to let go is important for you and your children.

Lastly, I do believe that not giving up on my son was the biggest factor that led to him returning back to his normal self. I think he was trying to test me, push me away, and see what I would do. See if I would quit on him. Ultimately, I don't know what it was, and probably never will, but I do believe allowing him the space to go through whatever he was going through and him knowing that I wasn't going anywhere allowed him to recover.

Be a good husband.

So much of what you do as a parent is passed on to your kids through how you act. The most impactful acts are likely to be those that come from how you interact with your spouse. When you show your child how much you love, care for, and respect their mother, you reflect the same on them. You also show them how a family can function. You show them the basics of what a relationship is and how it can make or break someone. As a parent, you are modeling the basic building blocks of life and society. So, it is ultra-important not to screw this part up. Having said that, in the next chapter I will cover how you can be the best husband you can be.

CHPT. 5:
HOW TO BE A GOOD HUSBAND

Be kind

First of all, you may not know *how* to be kind. You may not know what true kindness looks like or not have had it modeled for you appropriately. You may be living life thinking you are a kind person but, in reality, are not, and to little or no fault of your own. For example, you may think you are being kind to your spouse when in reality you are only being less mean than your father was to his spouse. It's possible you are still being abusive, angry, or mean, but to a lesser extent, and all because of your past, which has led you to view kindness differently.

It is important to gain an understanding of what real kindness is and looks like. But how do you determine if you are showing kindness in the way you should be? Well, it starts by understanding what kindness is and means. Kindness is simply this: *helping someone without expecting something in return.* Reread the "Kind" section in our list of characteristics of a good man if you need to.

Affection is another way to show kindness and you can show your affection for someone by using words or actions that let them know you really care about them. For example, you can tell someone they look nice, you can open the door for someone, you can ask a thoughtful question, you can buy a needed gift for someone, or just remind someone you love them by telling them so!

Kindness is much easier to define than to demonstrate sometimes, for sure, especially when you feel like you aren't getting your way or what you want. But showing kindness *consistently* is key to being a good husband. While kindness isn't about what you receive in return, I guarantee many wives would do just about anything for a husband who showed real kindness on a consistent basis. I'm sure many wives would appreciate a husband who would do even one helpful thing during the day, let alone multiple kind things, especially if their husbands expect nothing in return.

To summarize the point, being kind isn't about what you may or may not get in return. It is about doing *selfless* things that help or build up your spouse. And in most cases, kind behavior is often returned with kind behavior. So, do your best to show kindness consistently. And while you're at it, try to be kind more than once a day.

Sacrifice

Die to yourself. That's right, *die to yourself.* Forget *you*, forget your every little ache and complaint. Forget about all the little problems in your life, or all the little problems you have with your spouse, and stop. Stop and take a moment to step outside of yourself and think about what your spouse wants and needs. Take a mental inventory. Think about what *she* needs to feel more fulfilled. Think about what she *needs* to be a better person or to help her fulfill her purpose in life. And if you aren't sure, take the time to sit down with her and ask her. Ask her what things you can do to make her life more fulfilling. Ask her how you can work on yourself so you can strengthen your partnership. Ask her how you can help her elevate her life, rather than dragging it down. Ask her in what ways you may be hindering her ability to fulfill her purpose.

Just knowing you care enough about her to talk about these things should have a huge impact on her and your relationship. However, it will all be an empty gesture if you do not *follow through* with the acts of sacrifice you need to show.

Whether you end up sacrificing your time, money, energy, or whatever else it is you need to, the connection between you and your spouse should grow as a result.

Then get in the practice of sacrificing on a consistent basis. Don't just do something once and stop. Once you get into a habit of sacrificial behavior, periodically check back in with her. Check to see if there are parts of her life that have changed and need a new, fresh sacrificial approach from you.

This doesn't mean you can't continue to be a strong leader. It doesn't mean you can't, won't or shouldn't have your own needs met either. But sacrificing ensures you are doing the best you can for your partner, and doing the best for her is usually what is best for you both.

You are simply humbling yourself to understand your spouse's needs, and understanding her needs allows her to feel heard, appreciated, and loved. When she feels heard, appreciated, and loved, her spirits lift. And when she is elevated, it elevates you both. Having a sacrificial approach in marriage elevates love and connection through action and it is likely she will return the care and respect you are longing for.

Be on guard

Guard your spouse. Guard her honor. Guard her soul. Guard her spirit. Guard her body. Guard her children. Guard her parents. Guard her family. Guard all the things in her life that are important, even the things she may not see as having much importance at the time. Guard the obvious things in the obvious ways. But be on guard against the sneaky things too. The things that can creep into your life and marriage and steal it away. Sneaky things like sexual thoughts, images or feelings you, by nature, have for others. Instead, guard your sexuality for your spouse. Use your passion and desire to fuel your ability to guard her and feed into her life.

Have a level temperament

Relax. Pick your battles. Just as you do with your kids, let the little stuff go. Asking yourself specific questions can help. Questions like, is it important to "win" *every* argument? Is it worth destroying everything you are trying to build just so you can claim a "victory"? Is getting the "win" worth it if you lose *the one*?

I promise you, your anger and lack of emotional self-control will undermine *everything* good you want, whether it is for you, your family, or both, that is assuming you even consider what your family wants and what is in *their* best interest.

So, relax. Take a breath. Take another … and another. Breathe and think before you respond. Put every issue in the context of the "big picture." Learn to let some things go—otherwise how else can you grab the good things coming your way?

Be self-controlled

Sex, spending money, hobbies, sports, watching TV, playing video games, "time with the boys," are just some of the things most men want, or want to do, the most. None of these things are bad, but when they *consume* us, we've lost "us"—that is, the relationship between you and your spouse. These things easily contribute to you losing focus on what holds your family and your marriage together.

To do the things men love most while still maintaining a healthy marriage, men must learn to focus on balancing what they give and what they take. Good men must find a way to balance the happiness they get through the things they like to do with sacrifice and personal responsibility—the responsibility to grow in their character and nurture their marriage.

Take watching television, for example. You could allow yourself to watch TV all evening as soon as you get home from work. You could sit down and shut off your brain. Or you could set aside your desire to sit and watch TV and channel that desire into fulfilling your spouse's needs instead knowing that, in doing so, your spouse is going to grow happier and closer to you through your giving. You'll know that by being happier with you and closer to you, your spouse is more likely to help meet your needs, but remember, it isn't about what you might get in return. Anything you may get in return you must set aside. It is about demonstrating self-control to allow yourself to *give*.

By sacrificing and giving, you show yourself and your spouse that you *can* have self-control without demanding or expecting anything from her.

Continue to show self-control on a regular basis. Think about how it makes you feel the more you sacrifice and give. Analyze reactions, responses, and behavioral changes from your spouse. See if your life and hers change for the better. I bet it does, in a big way. Maybe not at first, but the more you do it the more likely it is to help. Stay consistent. Keep at it. Show restraint while feeding into your spouse and the other things that bring you happiness.

Listen then talk

In that order. Listen and *then* talk.

Let's tackle listening first.

Let's be real: most men struggle to listen. Most men struggle to listen and understand, specifically. We will listen to the game, the commentator, our buddy, our favorite TV show, our favorite movie, etc., but these are all passive ways in which we can listen, meaning it doesn't take much effort to hear these things. We don't have to think much about them other than hear them and let them pass through us. It does, however, take effort to hear and understand someone and it's what we need to do with our spouses.

Deepening the difficulty of listening is knowing how to respond after we've listened. We may listen but immediately think of how to fix the problem, and that is okay and natural for men. A problem arises when our spouse doesn't want a solution. They don't want us to fix anything at all. They want to be heard and understood. Political commentator Ben Shapiro has a great solution to this issue. Before he and his spouse get into a discussion, he begins by asking her, "Is this a listening conversation or a fixing conversation?" By doing this, from the get-go, he knows whether his spouse needs him to listen or if she is looking for a solution.

It is also important to understand the difference between passive and active listening. Passive listening is when you hear something but it tends to go in one ear and out the other. Retention and understanding with this approach is minimal, at best.

Active listening is hearing someone and then restating what they said back to them. Often, this is done in the form of asking a question or stating confirmation of what they said. You speak in a way that ensures they know you heard them and you understand or are looking for clarification if you don't understand.

While active listening is the best approach, it isn't easy for guys to do. I think it's why we like listening to games, shows, movies, etc. because we can be passive listeners in these cases. We can mentally "check out." Active listening takes much more effort. It requires focus on our part and engaging in a genuine act of listening and responding in conversation.

For example, your spouse may tell you they are really frustrated with work. As soon as you hear this, your first reaction should be to put down your phone down or turn off the TV and ask if they would like to talk about it. If they say yes, you ask if they need a listening ear or if they are looking for some solutions. From there, you can say things like, "What happened?", "I get your frustration, that would make me super frustrated too!" You can say simple things like, "Can you tell me more about that?" When your spouse is talking, you can say something like, "Well, if there is anything I can do, just let me know." And tell them, "I love you and I'm here for you!" Don't ignore them or pretend to listen. Don't get frustrated because they won't listen to what seems like an obvious fix to the problem in your view. Don't get annoyed because they have interrupted something you are doing either. Keep in mind what is most important and invest the time to *actively* listen.

Now, let's go over talking.

Talking may be as difficult, if not more difficult, for men than listening, depending on the issue. Talking about our sexual desires or other needs with our spouses? Nope. Not going to happen. Talking about our feelings? Nope! Talking in an understanding, empathetic, engaged, calm, or helpful way in response to our spouse's troubles or criticisms? Not likely.

Talking is difficult but absolutely necessary. And each topic we talk about requires tact, patience, and understanding. You must balance your message with your spouse's perspective in order for your words to have any impact.

For example: Let's say you have been feeling down lately. You have been struggling with feeling like you are coming up short at work, at home and in life generally. You may even suspect you are sliding into depression. Whatever it is, you know your attitude is negatively affecting many aspects of your life and your loved ones'.

In this instance, instead of letting your attitude and actions continue to decrease your quality of life and that of those around you, you say to your spouse one day, "Hey, I know this may sound a little crazy, but could we set aside some time to talk in the next couple weeks? I'm not sure if it's just me, or if you've noticed, but I have really been struggling lately and wanted to talk to you about what is going on."

My suspicion is if you do this, any good spouse will jump at the chance. Most spouses want the chance to have actual, *real* conversations with their husbands, eager to listen and help in any way they can.

Realize you don't have to talk about every single little thing. Nor do you need to. It is important to find a balance between the things you should handle on your own to protect others and the things you should talk to your spouse about. While most men don't want to show any sign of struggle or weakness and will bury everything, there are times when you need to talk. Work to share your mind and struggles more freely with your spouse. Finding this balance and the courage to talk is key.

I'll leave you with one final example. Let's say your spouse is talking to you about her no-good-very-bad day or her no-good-very-bad husband (yep, she's talking about you). Instead of checking out immediately, ignoring her completely, or mentally preparing your bombshell response before she has even finished speaking, you don't do anything. You keep your mouth shut and you just listen. Even for a few seconds after she finishes speaking, you take an extra moment to think. Then you say something like, "Hmm, okay, hang on a second, I need to think about that." Then, after filtering your response with your "is-my-response-going-to-make-her-mad" test, you respond with something like, "So you are saying (insert her concern here)?" "Could you tell me more about that/it?" Or, you say something like, "Dang, that sounds awful/horrible/frustrating/irritating/etc., is there anything I can do?" Or you say something like, "Hmm, I hear you saying (insert problem about *you* here). Is there anything I can do to help/improve?" The key here is to be humble, calm, patient, loving, kind, and empathetic. But the *absolute* #1 thing to do is this: if she asks you to do something or help with something… *DO IT*! Follow through.

Cherish her

Your wife is a gift. Be careful to treat her as such. Many men see their wives as a gift, a blessing, and a wonderful addition to their lives early in their relationship. During these times men are more romantic, treat their wives really well, and do everything they can to make sure they feel loved, appreciated and valued. Oftentimes, however, that vision and the associated acts of love become lost as time in the relationship goes on.

I want to challenge you to fight for the vision you first had of her. If you currently see her this way, keep it up! Either way, remember all the reasons why you love her and find her valuable. Remember and recognize all the good things about her and how uniquely special she is to you. Then tell her how you feel about her on a regular basis. Show her how you feel on a regular basis. Figure out what makes her feel loved most and do those things. Make a consistent effort to show her and remind her why she is the special gift in your life. Love her, care for her and show her you cherish her and every moment you are together!

CHPT. 6:

HOW PORNOGRAPHY POISONS MEN

I'll never forget the day pornography slapped me upside the head and imprinted on my mind forever.

I was 11 years old and in a tent in the yard of my friend's house. A few of my friends and I were camping outside for the night. My friend who lived at the house brought out some *Playboy* magazines his dad owned and showed them to us. As we lay there during that life-changing night, I remember just staring at the women in those magazines. I'm pretty sure my eyes were as wide open as they could possibly get. I'm not even sure I knew what I was looking at, but I do remember my mind and heart racing like crazy. The images I was looking at were lighting a fire inside me like I had never felt before.

It wasn't long after that night that the same friend showed me how to find pornographic images on the internet. His family had recently purchased a computer and this opened us up to a whole new world. While the internet and devices are everywhere today, at that time, computers and the internet were new.

Nearly everyone, including my family, was getting a computer and connecting to the internet. Once my family connected to the internet, my pornography viewing accelerated. The slow erosion of what should have been a beautiful understanding of sex and the relationship with it began.

It didn't seem like a big deal when I started to look at it. While I did feel some shame and guilt at times, I was just a kid coming into my teenage years. My hormones were raging. As nearly all boys at that age are, I was a wide-eyed, sexually charged kid. I was ready to devour every visual piece of "eye candy" I could. With the internet, I had quick and easy access to what felt like a never-ending candy store.

It didn't feel all that wrong either. My friends were doing it and encouraged it. It was talked about as if it was a normal and expected thing to do. At the time, it felt like I was fulfilling a normal sexual desire. I got to use what seemed like an endless amount of exciting visual stimulation to fulfill a natural desire. On top of that, I thought I was learning about sex in the process. But boy, was I WRONG.

As a kid, no one ever talked to me about a boy's sexual nature. No one told me how powerful it was and how important it was to control it. That was my biggest problem. No one helped me understand it or warned me how to control it and why. No one told me how much better off my psychological state and relationships would be if I controlled it, and man, do I wish someone would have.

Pornography consumption eventually became an addiction for me. I would look at it regularly and I got better and better at hiding it. I realized I was addicted after I heard a pastor say, **"Addiction is wanting more and more of something for less and less of a high."** That was me. I couldn't seem to end the cycle of temptation, consumption, and guilt. I wanted more and more of it while feeling less and less of a high each time I used it. Ultimately, the desire to turn pornographic fantasies into realities in my life ended my marriage.

I don't blame my parents for any of it though. In retrospect, I don't think anyone could have known the level of exposure one would have to porn once they had the internet. I don't think anyone really understood how easy it was to access pornographic content or how fast a person could dive into, and get lost in, an ocean of sexual distortion. While we may not have known then, we certainly know now. None of us can use that same excuse today.

Many of you reading this may not think looking at pornography is a problem. I get that. I also get that a lot of people believe looking at pornography is actually a *positive* thing. A *benefit* to themselves, their sex life, and relationships. I have heard this from people many times when I share my story, but I completely disagree. It may seem like a good thing now, but it is only a matter of time before it ruins something, if not everything. All I ask is for the opportunity to prove to you why porn is so harmful.

As you read the next section, allow me to present for you the case against using porn; why porn is very harmful to your brain, your body, your relationships and how you view and use sex. I will use objective evidence and very little opinion. If I cannot convince you to stop using porn, at least you will be much better informed. You will at least be able to make a more informed decision when deciding whether to use porn or not.

I will also make the case that *good men* don't look at pornography. Good men don't and shouldn't want to consume it and I will explain why. I will then outline what some of the great evils are as a result of using it and how good men can help end these evils by ending porn use. I will provide you with solutions; rational, realistic solutions to prevent or stop using porn.

"*Sex* is one of the greatest gifts to mankind. And *pornography* is a thief stealing that gift."

The Harmful Effects of Pornography

I don't think I need to try to convince any guy reading this that sex is a good thing. However, I do need to convince you of the part you may never have heard before; pornography *is* poisonous. It's poisonous to your partner, to you, to your family, and anything it touches. Don't try to kid yourself into believing otherwise, and don't let anyone else try to convince you otherwise either. Let me prove it to you.

Understand the scope of pornography. There are 40 *million* Americans that are regular visitors to porn sites. 70 percent of men aged 18 to 24 visit a porn site at least once per month. 35 percent of all online search engine requests relate to sex, about 68 million requests per day. 12 percent of all internet websites are pornographic and the average age of first exposure to porn is 11 years old with the largest consumer group of internet porn being men aged 35 to 49.[9] According to one study, 93 percent of boys are exposed to pornographic content before the age of 18.[5] What is the total value of an industry that large? Well, the estimated monetary value of the pornography industry is somewhere between six and 97 billion dollars.[1] Yes, *billion* dollars. There is no doubt the pornography industry is massive, far-reaching, and incredibly easy to access. So much so, it is practically inescapable.

Porn Sites Get More Visitors Each Month Than Netflix, Amazon, and Twitter Combined. http://www.huffingtonpost.com/2013/05/03/internet-por-stats_n_3187682.html (accessed February 15, 2020).

Second, understand the impacts of pornography on kids, adults, families, and sex. According to Patrick F. Fagan, Ph. D., psychologist and former Deputy Assistant Health and Human Services Secretary, "Among adolescents, pornography hinders the development of healthy sexuality, and among adults, it distorts sexual attitudes and social realities. In families, pornography use leads to marital dissatisfaction, infidelity, separation, and divorce." He also notes that, "Two recent reports, one by the American Psychological Association on hypersexualized girls, and the other by the National Campaign to Prevent Teen Pregnancy on the pornographic content of phone texting among teenagers, make clear that the digital revolution is being used by younger and younger children to dismantle the barriers that channel sexuality into family life."[8]

The following are other negative effects of porn:

1. Those who frequently consume internet pornography are less likely to marry because they see pornography as a marital sexual gratification substitute.[2]
2. The more pornography a man watches the more he needs to conjure images of pornography to maintain arousal. He

will be more likely to ask for particular sexual acts with his partner as a result. He will also have more concerns over his sexual performance and body image.[7]

3. Extramarital sex is one of the most commonly cited reasons for divorce and pornography consumption correlates with positive attitudes towards extramarital affairs.[10]
4. Researchers believe pornography's intense stimulation of the brain causes significant changes to it, similar to those experienced with drug addiction.[6]
5. As hours of reported pornography use increase, the amount of grey matter in the brain decreases.[2] And if you are familiar with human anatomy and physiology at all, this should scare the living hell out of you, so to speak.

"Individuals who never view sexually explicit material report higher relationship quality and lower rates of infidelity than those who do."[4]

Those are only *some* of the low-lights in regards to how pornography negatively impacts people. For an even more comprehensive look at the negative side effects of pornography, check out the "*Harmful Effects of Pornography Reference Guide*" from Fight the New Drug at fightthenewdrug.org. This resource is research based and is nearly 100 pages long. I hope you see the clear harmful effects pornography has on people's lives. It doesn't just impact you and those closest to you; it also fuels what are some of the world's most harmful effects on people *outside* of you and those closest to you. These people, and the industries and issues they deal with, must be mentioned. Things like human sex trafficking and sex abuse. Things like abortion. Each devastating in its own way for the victims (to say the very least). Diseases like sexually transmitted diseases, the spread of which is made much worse when having multiple sex partners—a desire driven to an even greater degree by pornography consumption.

The good news is each of these things could be obliterated if all men were good men. Good men who understood these issues, knew how to stop them, wanted to stop them, and did.

CHPT. 7:
HOW GOOD MEN CAN END PROBLEMS AND EVILS RELATED TO SEX

Sexually Transmitted Diseases

One of the biggest problems destroying the sexual experience is sexually transmitted diseases. These diseases are better known by the acronym "STDs" and are spread through sexual intercourse. That includes oral, vaginal, and anal. Each STD is a very real and important issue to consider when deciding how you are going to engage in sex. Many men don't know about them or know very little about them. So, why is it important to know about these diseases? Because they are harmful to your health, your sexual activity and your sexual partner's health.

Let's talk about the three most common STDs in the United States. They are syphilis, gonorrhea and chlamydia.

Syphilis is characterized by sores on the genitals, rectum, or mouth. Through stages of progression, it can lead to damage of your brain, nerves, eyes, heart, blood vessels, liver, bones, and joints.[4] Gonorrhea is characterized by an infection of the genitals, rectum, or throat. This infection can lead to significant discomfort and abnormal discharges in these areas.[2] Chlamydia is often symptomless and so is often left untreated. It can sometimes lead to pain and discharges from the reproductive organs. Chlamydia can even impair a woman's ability to get pregnant and cause ectopic pregnancies, which can be deadly.[1]

As of 2018, there were more than 115,000 syphilis cases, 580,000 gonorrhea cases (highest number reported since 1991), and 1.7 million chlamydia cases (the most ever reported to the Centers for Disease Control).[3] And that only covers the three most common STDs. There are many others.

How does the CDC recommend avoiding STDs? They say, and I quote, "The only way to avoid STDs is to not have vaginal, anal, or oral sex." We all know that isn't going to happen forever. Everyone is likely to, at one point or another, engage in a sexual activity. We need to know how best to prevent contracting and spreading these diseases. The CDC makes another recommendation to address this. They recommend to "be in a long-term mutually monogamous relationship with a partner who has been tested and has negative STD results." To be clear, mutually monogamous meaning you and your partner are only having sex with each other.

Finally, remember these diseases can be transmitted to a baby during delivery. These diseases can cause anywhere from minimal to severe health issues for the child. The problems related to these diseases can go beyond affecting just you and your sexual partner. Be smart. Don't be selfish. Know the risks for *everyone* involved when you decide to have sex outside of a "mutually monogamous relationship."

Human Sex Trafficking

Human sex trafficking involves the use of force, fraud, or coercion to obtain some type of labor or commercial sex act.[4] Why do I bother mentioning this in a book intended to describe what it means to be a good man? Because good men fight evil and human sex trafficking is evil. Can you think of a worse evil than forced, fraudulent, or coerced sex slavery, especially when so many victims are children? I can't.

It is important to talk about how the pornography and sex trafficking industries fuel one another as well and to talk about how good men, who stop consuming porn, can make a significant difference in ending the sex trafficking industry.

Let's start by *trying* to understand the scope of the sex trafficking industry.

As of 2016, 4.8 million people out of 40 million victims of modern slavery were victims of sexual slavery. 99 percent of those were female and one in every five victims was a child. Due to the difficulty of detecting victims, especially with children, the actual counts of victims are likely much higher.[1] According to the "2010 Trafficking in Persons Report" by the U.S. Department of State, only .4 percent of victims are identified. *Only .4 percent.*

How does using pornography fuel the human trafficking industry? Many of the victims of sex trafficking are forced to make pornographic material. They are forced to re-enact specific acts from pornographic material consumed by their captors. Sex slaves are often taught "how to perform" via pornographic material.[2] Of course, there are the more obvious connections as well, like porn consumption increasing the temptation of consumers to turn fantasy into reality by purchasing sex. Each industry adds to the other industries' profitability.

It is estimated that the human sex trafficking industry is worth *150 billion dollars*,[3] much of which is fueled by the fantasy and perversion of porn use. An industry that, remember, is worth upwards of 97 billion dollars itself, a lot of which comes from the exploitation of human trafficking victims.

It is clear that the pornography and human sex trafficking industries are intimately linked. And each can end when good men *end the demand* for both.

Abortion

Abortion is defined as "The termination of a pregnancy after, accompanied by, resulting in or closely followed by the *death* of the *embryo or fetus* (emphasis added). Such as, 1) the spontaneous expulsion of a human fetus during the first 12 weeks of gestation, 2) induced expulsion of a human fetus, and/or 3) expulsion of a fetus by a domestic animal often due to infection at any time before completion of pregnancy."[1]

A fetus is defined as "An unborn or unhatched vertebrate especially after attaining the basic structural plan of its kind specifically: a developing human from usually two months after conception to birth."[3]

You and I were a fetus at one point in our lives. Not one of us could have gotten here if we hadn't been there. Abortion snuffs out a life, a fetus, one that has the potential to go anywhere and be anything. It ends a life that will never even be aware of the opportunity taken from it. It ends a life that will never get the chance to fight for the right to its own life and opportunity.

As I continue to talk about abortion, I want to be clear I will be referring to #2 in the above definition, "the induced expulsion of a human fetus." Or, to put it in simpler terms, the purposeful killing of a human fetus. I will also be referring to abortions of *unwanted* fetuses—fetuses killed when the mother's life is *not* in danger, not fetuses that die as a result of an accident or health condition. With all that said, I mention abortion because good men should protect innocent human life. They should do all they can to prevent the taking of innocent human life too. And it doesn't get much more innocent than defenseless humans in a mother's womb.

Is abortion a widespread issue? Absolutely. There were 623,741 *reported* legal abortions performed in the U.S. in 2016.[2] Worldwide, the estimation is there are 25 million *unsafe* abortions performed each year.[4] These numbers don't even consider the number of "safe" abortions or unreported abortions. That is a lot of life being lost and most, if not all, abortions would end if good men would practice abstinence until they were in a mutually monogamous sexual relationship.

It is obvious, but still noteworthy, to point out that good men who practice abstinence will not be getting anyone pregnant. Avoiding pregnancy is the easiest way to prevent unintended pregnancy and abortion. (I talk more about *practical* solutions for how to practice abstinence later.)

Once a good man is in a committed relationship, he and his spouse are much more likely to family plan. Family planning means you talk to your spouse about whether you want to have kids or not. Family planning can help reduce abortion rates due to the reduction in the incidence of unintended pregnancies. And again, what do unintended pregnancies often lead to?

Unwanted children and the abortion of them. Even if a good man does not family plan but is in a committed relationship, he is much more likely to stick around and help raise his child, expected or not.

The whole idea is simple: if a man doesn't have sex, pregnancy won't occur and when he does, he should do it while in a committed relationship. A committed relationship where both people discuss whether or not to have children. That way they can do their best to avoid unwanted pregnancies and the chance they abort their child. Whether you are "pro-life" or "pro-choice," this is one thing I hope everyone can agree to. Abstinence and monogamous sexual relationships can literally save lives.

Millions of unborn humans are dying every year unnecessarily. And unless you see abortion as the means to a sexually liberated lifestyle's end, you should see it as being easily preventable and make the sacrifice to save lives.

Yes, saving lives is a great benefit of sexual discipline and commitment, but there are a lot of other benefits for couples who share the incredible gift of sex only with each other. While I have talked about abstinence and committed relationships repeatedly, these are easy things to talk about but not easy things to do. Not. At. All. So, in the next chapter I propose solutions for how boys can grow up to be good men through abstinence and sexual monogamy, all while achieving maximum sexual fulfillment.

CHPT. 8:

HOW TO GET THE MOST OUT OF SEX

This section can be used as a framework for learning (if you have not yet had sex) or learning what one should understand and guard as it relates to sex to get the most fulfillment out of it. It can also be used as a guide to teaching yourself or teaching your son about sex. It can help guide either of you along a path towards a better understanding of how to think of, and engage in, sexual activity.

From the ages of 6–12*, in an age-appropriate manner, your parents, guardians or trusted adults in your life carefully increase your understanding of:*

1. What your body's "private parts" are.
2. Why it is important to protect your "private parts."

3. What sex is.
4. What "tricky people" are and ways they trick children into doing inappropriate things.
5. What is "inappropriate" sexual behavior, touching, talking, etc.
6. What to do in cases where tricky people may try inappropriate things with them.
7. Why and how to start training your eyes, heart, and mind away from inappropriate things.

From the ages of 13–19 *your parent increases your understanding of:*

1. How men view sex *generally* and their increased desire for it.
2. How women look at sex *generally* and their typical desire for intimacy.
3. How beautiful and incredible the gift of sex can be. And how sex is much more likely to be a gift, rather than a curse, when shared between two people who are committed to each other.
4. How many—innumerable—sexual traps there are in this world, like pornography.
5. The lie that sex with many partners is liberating and fulfilling.
6. Strategies to ensure you have the most fulfilling sex life possible such as:

    ✧ Training your eyes *away* from as much sexual imagery as possible. This reduces your visual sexual expectations. It also allows you to visually *consume* the one person you were intended to be with—not everything else you may find enticing—and have an understanding that this will take time, self-discipline, and determination.

- ✧ Training your mind to think thoughts as clean as possible. This will reduce many unrealistic sexual expectations. This will also preserve your lustful thoughts and sexual desires for your spouse. The one they were meant to be for. Thoughts and desires that should be shared confidently and trustfully with the person you are going to spend the rest of your life with.
- ✧ How to use moral, clean, and healthy strategies to achieve—or avoid altogether—sexual release. More on this in the following sections.

After age 20:

1. Stay patient, committed, and wait for sex with your spouse.

Let's unpack all of this information a bit.

Maybe you meet the one person you intend to spend the rest of your life with quickly.

Maybe you don't. Either way, let's say you practice training your eyes, mind, and body as you grow into adulthood. You aren't always perfect, but you have done a really good job at it. You've done your best to stay true to your desire to experience sex with your spouse only. You've done your best to preserve for yourself experiencing every ounce of fulfillment from sex you can by waiting for that one, special person.

Imagine, after patiently waiting all that time, you *do* find your spouse. Isn't it logical to believe fulfillment from sex in this circumstance would be really high, rather than engaging in a series of one-night stands?

What if we add to this relationship? The one where you have waited to have sex with one another and you are both morally compatible as well. You share the same values and share the same hopes and dreams for your lives. Really take a minute to imagine a relationship like this—one in which you both trained your bodies, minds, and hearts for each other and the moment when you share the gift of sex together. My bet, and I'm pretty sure it is a safe one, is the sexual fireworks would be out of this world!

But for those who might ask, and rightfully so, "How do you know this would be true?" Well, I *don't* know for certain. But follow my logic for a minute as to why I think it would be. Let me start by asking you a question. Is someone who has built their sexual *expectations* off of what they've seen in pornography, the latest rap video, or any number of a million sexualized images—only to be disappointed when sex in real life never matches these expectations—more or less likely to have a great sex life? Or is it more likely that a person who's seen none of that, only their partner, and *consumes* only their partner is going to have a better sex life?

Again, imagine for a minute this kind of relationship. Imagine this kind of *sexual* relationship. Imagine a committed relationship with an untainted sex life. One where the two of you share, grow and explore each other without any outside influences. One where only the two of you—fueled by your love, shared values, focus on each other, communication and commitment—enjoy the gift of sex without any of the worldly perversion poisoning it. This is what we should all strive for.

This is the goal for those of you who have not yet had sex and would like to get the most out of it someday. For those of you who have already become sexually active and do not find it fulfilling, ask yourself if the topics outlined earlier in this chapter had been taught to you, and at the age and pace recommended, would your sex life be better today? If you find yourself believing that might be the case, consider reevaluating your life and sex life and commit yourself to retraining your brain. Commit your life towards entering into a committed sexual relationship someday. While it may never be untainted completely because of your past, it can certainly be better than how things are currently, chasing one-night stands and momentary sexual pleasure in whatever form(s)!

A large and important question now remains and must be addressed. "How can I wait for sex when every part of my being is urging me to have sex, nearly all the time?" Well, this is a question I will address in the next chapter.

CHPT. 9:
HOW TO WAIT FOR SEX

Frankly, this is the most difficult portion of this book I have had to write. It is the one I spent the most time on, edited the most, and modified whole sections of, multiple times. Why do I bother to tell you this? Because my time spent on this topic speaks to the difficulty we all have when it comes to talking about waiting for sex. A topic *many* people won't see the point in talking about at all, especially in an age where sexual promiscuity is so celebrated. Many people don't see the need to put limits on their sex life and that's their decision, but the consequences of that lifestyle can be severe. By this point in the book, I hope you see the clear benefits of waiting and the consequences of not.

While the options to wait for sex are straightforward in my view, it doesn't make them any easier to talk about. Most people shy away from talking about the subject, and understandably so. Let's dive right into the first, albeit brief, option as it relates to how to wait for sex.

Perfect Purity

This is the ideal. To maintain a perfectly pure mind and pure heart, guarding your eyes from seeing anything perverted and refraining from any sexual release of any kind. Sounds easy, right? HA! Nope, not even remotely. However, it needs to be said. It needs to be brought up because there is nothing wrong with pursuing perfection, certainly as it relates to sexual purity. Purity is a beautiful thing and is something everyone should strive for. There is nothing wrong, and there should be nothing seen as wrong, with saving *every* sexual fiber of who you are for your spouse.

The "A" Word: Abstinence

Abstinence is when you do not engage in sexual activity, of any kind, with another person. While perfect purity would certainly fall into this category, it is important to realize you can still fall into a trap while abstaining from sex. One that can continually distort your image of sex.

The trap I am talking about happens when you crave and fantasize about perverted sexual acts and with multiple partners. While you may be doing this and not having any sexual contact with another person, you are doing serious damage to your thoughts, perceptions, and expectations of sex. Are you abstaining from sex with another in this instance? Yes. Are you doing yourself any favors as it relates to sex, how you view sex, and the health of your future sexual relationship? No!

It is so important for men to guard their eyes, hearts, and minds when it comes to sex. This includes the period of time abstaining from sex. It isn't easy, I know. We are visual creatures and most men build expectations by playing out sexual imagery in our minds, but the healthiest form of abstinence is one in which we guard all parts of our sexual being, especially the parts between the ears, our brains. That leads us into our last and most difficult to talk about option.

The "M" Word: Masturbation

Yes, I know. I don't want to talk about this, and I know you don't want to talk about this either. I was squirming and uncomfortable when I wrote this and I am sure you are squirming and uncomfortable as you are reading this. No one wants to talk about it. Heck, even the internet doesn't want to talk about it. In doing my research for this section, when I typed in "benefits of masturbation," in all the search engines I tried the autofill never went past "benefits of mast." So, you know this is a tough subject to discuss if even Google doesn't want a part of it. Even more than masturbation though, I want to talk about an idea called "meditative masturbation."

So aside from asking yourself why I am bringing this subject up at all, you might also be asking yourself, why "meditative"? I will address both these important questions in the next sections. First, let's address why I bring this topic up at all.

Mental peace, sexual peace, optimal sexual fulfillment, and the importance of maintaining a healthy, monogamous sexual relationship is why I bring this up. No matter how much it may make us squirm to think about discussing this subject, and no matter how embarrassing it may be, it is still something we *desperately* need to talk about, especially as it relates to helping you become a good man and adult boys become good men so they can enjoy and protect their sexuality.

"But how," you may ask, "can this help me become a good man?" Because meditative masturbation may be the best, most realistic tool to preserve sexual fulfillment with your spouse someday. It may be the best way to prevent mental perversion and lay the groundwork for a healthy, monogamous relationship in the future, especially since monogamy is the best way to get the most out of sex and relational satisfaction.[2]

At the very least, this approach should be seen as a *credible option* to preserve optimal sexual fulfillment while you wait. If "perfect purity" isn't achievable this could be seen as the next best option for those who are waiting. Because let's face reality, the majority of you will not be perfect or pure all the time. Expecting yourself to be perfect would be like expecting the sun not to rise. Overall, you need to know more than what you've figured out on your own as it relates to these topics.

Physiologically, masturbation can lead to health benefits such as lowering your risk of prostate cancer[3], promoting sleep, promoting the release of endorphins (the natural chemical produced in the body that causes physical and mental well-being), and reducing stress[1]. But, if used in an improper way—as it is often used when viewing pornography—there are likely to be fewer benefits. Likely, it is to your harm. For example, when consuming porn, the brain does mental gymnastics fantasizing and creating unrealistic expectations regarding what you are consuming. It's all done in an effort to achieve sexual release but attached with it are many negative—often mental—consequences.

So, how do you use masturbation as a tool for sexual release *without* the mental distortion of pornography as a stimulus? This is where the meditation piece comes in and where guilt-free, healthy sexual release can lie.

But *how* do you achieve this exactly? Well, the first step in the process is to simply realize you don't *need* the usual internal and external sources you rely on for sexual arousal. You learn to separate the two from each other. If you are not sexually active yet, you would focus on preventing yourself from relying on internal and external sources of sexual stimulation simply by knowing what they are and how to avoid them. These would be things like fantasies.

Fantasies are the internal sources of stimulation that arouse you through your thoughts about sex. You could think of these as the movies you play in your mind and they involve your sexual desires. These are where you develop your sexual expectations too. Now, external sources, on the other hand, are things that arouse you through your senses. For men, most of these are visual.

Now that you understand this framework of how we typically associate arousal with release, do a self-assessment. Think about what kind of stimulation *you* rely on for your sexual arousal and release. Determine if any of them are pure and/or unrealistic. Then, once you have determined your sources of arousal, you can stop the inappropriate ones. By doing this you can eliminate your expectations, perverted input, and shift towards a clearer mind instead.

The second step in the process is to then start practicing the meditation piece. Think of meditation as shutting your brain down to focus on one thing. It is in this mental space that you can focus on keeping the perverted thoughts out.

Over time, it is reasonable to believe you will gain greater mental peace and overall sexual health. Your unrealistic sexual expectations begin to go away. Any insecurity from you or your partner begins to go away as well since you are no longer comparing each other to anything sexually. You can both focus on each other rather than external, poisonous influences.

CHPT. 10:

HOW TO BE A FIGHTER

I'll never forget the time in my life when I became a fighter.

After I divorced in 2015, life circumstances led to me filing for custody of our two children. They were seven and four years old at the time. We went through the typical legal proceedings and participated in what's called a custody study. For those who don't know what a custody study is, it is when a third, trained party investigates you, your ex-spouse, and your children's lives. Based on their investigation, they recommend to the court which parent should have custody. It is a long, painstaking and intrusive process.

What were the results of ours? Let's just say the custody study didn't go my way—and it wasn't even close. Even though

I was confident the recommendation would come out in my favor and the evaluator would recommend I had custody, I was wrong.

Once knowing the custody evaluator's findings, while I felt I had ample reason to fight them I decided not to go to trial. I was ready to move on with my life. I was tired of fighting and ready for peace, consistency, and stability in our lives. Most importantly, it was recommended I get half-time with the kids, which was my main goal, and I wasn't willing to risk losing that. In anticipation of peace and increased time with my kids, I surrendered legal custody and shut my mouth. I was certain peace would reign in all our lives. I was certain we would all move forward. But I was wrong, very wrong.

As soon as we settled into our new agreement, things went sideways. I began to receive near constant accusations. Accusations I was a physical, emotional, and sexual abuser. Later, accusations began to be made that I had been and still was physically, emotionally, and sexually abusing the kids. I often felt like I was living in one reality—*the actual reality*—while my accusers were living in another. It was as if my accusers were living in their own version of "the upside-down" from the Netflix show *Stranger Things*, only it was our lives superimposed in the setting.

During this time, I was doing my best to keep the kids' lives as stable as possible. I put selfish desires aside and just focused on my kids. I determined within myself to fight for their mental, spiritual, and physical growth, all the while being continually perceived as doing the opposite by my accusers. All the while beginning to sense my kids were starting to distance themselves from me. All the while I could see their love and trust for me beginning to waver due to reasons and influences outside my control. But I refused to quit. I continued to fight.

I wanted nothing more than to just enjoy my time with my kids and be left alone. I wanted to do the best job I could still do by being a good dad—filling the gaps where I felt my own father had failed—and be as involved in their lives as much as I could. Even in the midst of my own broken family. Even in the midst of imperfect circumstances. None of that mattered or was even acknowledged as remotely truthful by my accusers. It felt like they simply wanted me to be destroyed, at whatever cost necessary. While they may well have wanted me to quit, I refused to. I was going to let love, persistence, and my presence overcome the situation the kids and I were in.

After a little over a year of direct verbal accusations, I received some helpful clarity. A person familiar with my situation told me I was likely dealing with what's called "parental alienation." It seemed to fit our situation exactly and as I learned about it, I gained some much-needed perspective. I gained some tools in that moment to help me fight.

By the end of 2018, accusations made against me became so severe that Child Protective Services, the local police, and attorneys became regular parts of my life as I fended off each accusation of abuse. Each instance presented a great challenge in my life. But each instance gave me opportunities to grow as a man, to grow as a fighter, and that is exactly what I did.

The result of the first major accusation made against me (to the authorities) was without question the most difficult time in my life. Why? Because it led to 109 days when I would not see or speak to my kids. 109 days of not knowing when I would see them again. 109 days of not knowing how they were doing or how they were feeling. 109 days knowing they were somewhere, but somewhere I couldn't find them. Somewhere I couldn't hug them. Somewhere I couldn't tell them I loved them or was thinking about them. Not without supervision anyway; that would come later.

I eventually saw my kids for two supervised visits before the police cleared me of all allegations. Each visit was heart-wrenching and I wouldn't wish that experience on any loving parent. It was nearly enough to make me, and I would imagine anyone else, feel like giving up. There is really no good way to describe the pain associated with watching your kids treat you like the devil your accusers claim you are. Watching them ignore you. Watching them as they keep their distance, wanting nothing to do with you. Watching them exist in their "upside down" world. There is no good way to describe the mental gymnastics one goes through when trying to understand why the kids are acting the way they are, what got them to a point where their behavior doesn't reflect reality. But I still didn't give up; on them or us. I continued to fight with whatever legal means I could. Once I was cleared of the accusations made against me, I was given my normal time back *plus* the time I had lost with them during those 109 days and moved on. Unfortunately, the need to fight would arise again quickly. Even though I had made it through an incredible trial, the depths of which I never thought my will, faith or mental strength would be tested, I had to fight again.

Not long after this incident, the accusations began again. As did the alienation. Because of this and explicit threats to take the kids away from me by my accusers I felt I had no choice. I had to fight. I filed for custody again in hopes to get some real stability for my kids, hopefully for good this time. But the fight wouldn't be easy. The accusations and alienation got so bad that yet another complaint was filed with the authorities against me but this time *in the middle of* a second custody study by a parental alienation expert. Thankfully, I was quickly cleared this time, but it didn't make the fight any easier. I still lost 10 days with my kids before I could try to pick them up again. And when I did try I was simply refused my time with them and had to pursue further legal recourse to get my time with them back. I would go another 59 days without seeing my kids.

By December 2019, I had my time back and another round of make-up days to compensate me for days I lost. But the fight *still* wasn't over. In the winter and spring of 2020, COVID-19 hit the world and shut everything down, including the courts. Court dates were postponed and what seemed like a long process to determine custody became even longer.

Even though I felt like things would never end, and I was living in a perpetual state of "guilty until proven innocent," I refused to quit. I continued to fight. I knew my kids needed me in their lives. I knew they needed my leadership. I knew they needed my direction. I knew they needed my presence. And it didn't matter what the cost to me was. It didn't matter how much time it took. It didn't matter how much energy, emotional toll, stress, or worry I needed to endure. All that mattered was I was fighting for what I knew was right, good, and just for our children. And at the end of the day, when all was said and done, I wanted to be able to look back on this time and at least say, "I did *everything* I could," and have my children be able to look back and say, "Dad did everything he could." Even if I lost, I could sleep at night knowing I did everything I could.

But I didn't lose. The kids didn't lose. Our court case and custody study eventually continued and I was awarded custody. Later, I would even have my kids living with me full-time.

I had fought. I had persevered. I had grown. I had learned. I didn't quit. I never gave up. And through the raw, deep pains of missing all the time I did with my kids, I learned to have a much greater appreciation for my time with them when I did get to be with them. It led to an awareness of how important *each moment* we have together is, how important living in the moment with my kids is, and how living in the moment with them has led to some incredible times, incredible moments, and a relationship with them that allows me the best opportunity to shape them into good human beings. All things that likely would never have happened, or at least not as impactfully so, had I not fought.

How to be a fighter

How do good men fight, especially when so many of the characteristics of a good man tend to come across as the "sensitive" kind? Well, a good man needs to know when, or how, to abandon sensitivity and fight. A good man needs to know when to fight while remaining sensitive and when to fight without being sensitive. Finding the right amount of both—or neither—depending on the fight, is key. For example, the softer traits would not apply at all to a physical fight. For example, a physical fight involving a good man who is protecting his family, if their lives were in danger, can't involve sensitivity. In a mental or verbal fight, however, it is likely you will need to rely on more of the "sensitive" traits to be an effective fighter. The point is good men should know when to sharpen, rather than soften, the edges of their character and go to war and know what amount of both is required to win the fight at hand.

Here are three ways to approach fighting any battle:

Get up

Yeah, that's right. GET UP. Get off your butt and stop feeling sorry for yourself. Stop playing the same self-defeating recording over and over again in your head. You know, the one that keeps telling you that you can't do it. The one telling you it isn't worth it. The one that keeps telling you it would just be easier if you didn't. The one that keeps convincing you things are fine just the way they are.

Listen to me. If you think to yourself, *I don't feel like it,* you won't. If you think to yourself, *I'll never make it,* you won't. If you think, *I'm not good enough,* remember *you're not.* But you can *go, do,* and *be* better. But you have to get up. You have to get up and put in the work.

So instead of defeating yourself, *get up* and start *making* something of yourself. Start "feeling like it" and suck it up. Start by doing one positive thing today. Read something positive. Invest in something positive that makes you and those around you better.

I promise you, the work you put in *is* worth it. Your kids are worth it. Your spouse is worth it. Your family is worth it. Your financial stability is worth it. Your future generations are worth it. *YOU* are worth it. So, get up. Figuratively, literally or both. Whatever it is you need to do to take that first step towards going somewhere positive in your life, *do it now.* Seriously. Put this book down, or press pause on the audio if you're listening to this, and do one thing now to fight for your goals. Maybe that first thing is setting some goals. Maybe you need to start by making a list of life priorities or finding your meaning or purpose in life. Whatever it is, *get up* and start fighting.

Show up

You lose 100% of the fights you don't show up for. So, once you have a goal or goals, or you have clear priorities set for your life, *show up* for them. Every day, show up. Do at least one thing a day to fight for what you want or what you know others need. Whatever it is, show up to the fight. Don't quit a fight you've started and don't keep avoiding the fight you've been too gutless or lazy to show up for in the first place. No regrets. No second guesses. *Show up* and fight.

Throw up

Seriously, throw up. Yes, I am literally talking about vomiting. Okay, okay, no, you don't need to actually throw up, so let me explain. Have you ever exercised to the point where you have either thrown up or felt like you were going to? Well, that is the level of intensity you must be willing to go to in order to achieve your goals.

To be a fighter—a *winner*—you have to go so hard sometimes, so deep within yourself during the process that the work reveals good parts of you—parts you didn't even know were accessible. And after all that work, once you've thrown up a few times, you begin to realize how much of yourself you have to offer. You begin to realize how much you *are* capable of. And you realize how much more of yourself you may still have left to give.

Now, for those of you who may be thinking, *Okay, that sounds great, Justin, but what happens when I have more race left to run and I've "thrown up"? I don't have anything left to give.* Well, that's what teammates are for.

It is the times when you've done everything you can and "run out of gas" when you'll need to call on your teammates. Your "teammates," are your closest friends, family, mentors, and other allies. If you don't have any teammates, you better get some because you *will* need them. If you don't, maybe that should be the first thing you fight for. Make some friends, reconnect with family, or find a mentor because these need to be the people who know your goals, know where your finish line is, and are willing to come alongside you to pick you up when you fall. These should be the people who know where your finish line is, hand you a bucket to puke in, and help carry you until you've either finished the fight or recovered enough to continue the fight on your own.

Maybe your fight is to be present for your kids. Maybe your fight is to end generational curses in your family. Maybe your fight is to save your marriage. Maybe your fight is to get healthy or stop viewing pornography. Maybe your fight is to end an addiction. Whatever your fight is, you MUST be willing to "throw up" to win it. And having teammates around you to help you, push you, and hold you accountable can help get you there. So, *get up, show up, throw up,* and fight.

CHPT. 11: HOW TO HANDLE ADVERSITY AND DEPRESSION

A good man should be able to recognize adversity and depression when he experiences them. A good man should be able to acknowledge adversity when it occurs and know how to resolve any depression that comes as a result. Why? Because knowing how to recognize it and deal with it can lead to a *much* better and happier life for you *and* your loved ones. That being said, and let me be clear, this is *not* an easy thing to do and cannot always be done on your own. Adversity and depression can be overwhelming and feel impossible to overcome. But just because adversity and depression are difficult to deal with doesn't mean we should ignore them. Their difficulty should only highlight the importance of overcoming them, which should make you all the more resolved to tackle them.

Let's face it, adversity and depression are inevitable in life. Much of it ends up manifesting as a lack of emotion and/or anger. And many of the world's evils occur when guys lose control because they don't know how to handle either. Many men don't even realize they are experiencing depression until it's too late. Too late to save the quality of their life. Too late to save the quality of their loved ones' lives. Too late to fix the damage caused by heavy mental burdens leading to the destructive behavior.

I know this because I have lived this myself. There was a time in my life when, while not formally diagnosed, I believe I dealt with depression [The American Psychiatric Association states, "Depression (major depressive disorder) is a common and serious medical illness that negatively affects how you feel, the way you think and how you act."[2]]

For me, it felt like I was in the middle of a pit of quicksand. As time went on, I slipped deeper and deeper into the pit. One rejection here, another there, a lost family member, one failed life expectation after another, failed purposes, and crushing losses all pulled me deeper into the darker places within me.

For most people, depression continues until they have enough negative experiences—real or imagined—that push them over the edge. Eventually, many people give up completely and commit suicide, *especially men*. How do I know this? Because between the years 2008–2018, 460,076 people committed suicide and 359,080 of those were male. *Nearly 80%* of all the suicides during this 10-year span were men. During this same 10-year time span, suicide was so prevalent for men that it was the seventh leading cause of death, just below diabetes. Suicide didn't even register (thankfully) in the top 10 causes of death for women.[3]

The men who don't commit suicide live with suffering and few recognize they have a problem and get help. I thank God I was finally able to recognize I had a problem and got help. I hope reading this allows you to do the same. But healing first begins with recognition.

Recognizing depression isn't easy, especially recognizing it on your own and as it relates to you. But awareness is the key to change. So, it is important to understand the signs and symptoms of depression. According to the Mayo Clinic, symptoms of major depression may include:

- Feelings of sadness, tearfulness, emptiness or hopelessness
- Angry outbursts, irritability or frustration, even over small matters
- Loss of interest or pleasure in most or all normal activities, such as sex or hobbies
- Sleep disturbances, including insomnia or sleeping too much
- Tiredness and lack of energy, so even small tasks take extra effort
- Reduced appetite and weight loss or increased cravings for food and weight gain
- Anxiety, agitation or restlessness
- Slowed thinking, speaking or body movements
- Feelings of worthlessness or guilt, fixating on past failures or self-blame
- Trouble thinking, concentrating, making decisions and remembering things
- Frequent or recurrent thoughts of death, suicidal thoughts or attempts

- Unexplained physical problems, such as back pain or headaches

With depression, you may appear to others as fine on the outside, but on the inside you feel like you are up to your neck in darkness. You can find yourself not enjoying *anything*. You can feel pressure all around you and not know how any of it got there. You can feel like you are in a dark pit of your own and not know how, or if, you will ever get out. Unfortunately, some people don't get out. Some people remain stuck. Some people allow the last shove from life to push them over the edge and they leave this world. Don't be that person. Recognize what you are feeling and get help. Remember depression, despair, and unhappiness are all parts of life and virtually everyone will experience them to different degrees. But while it may be inevitable, it *can* be overcome, but it *takes work*.

So, what does overcoming depression look like? Well, in my experience, getting out of my pit of quicksand went something like this: I first had to make a choice, to fight or give up. Once I made the decision to fight, as cliché as it sounds, I simply took one step at a time from there. I took one moment at a time. I took one fight at a time. I took one day at a time. I worked at making sure I was able to talk about or write down how I was feeling. I worked at expressing my feelings as authentically as I could to myself or others. I worked to make myself, my brain and my heart lighter. Eventually, the pressure started lifting and so did I.

Another thing that helped me was learning from others. I started to listen to and read books by people and philosophers who seemed to have a common-sense grasp on the human condition. I learned all I could from them. I learned how human beings can work and choose to be happy, how to handle adversity, disappointment, abuse, loss, and the variety of difficulties in life. As time passed, I continued to get lighter and lighter. Mentally, I became stronger and eventually I was out of my pit of despair. While I would like to tell you I am happy *all* the time now and you will be happy all the time if you work at it, it isn't true. Is it possible? Sure. I can see how it may be possible, but for the majority of people, it isn't realistic. Because struggles *will* come. Disappointments *will* come. The world is full of both just waiting to trip you up, hoping you'll fall down.

For me, the struggle for happiness and fulfillment has been like walking up a sandy mountain. At the top of the mountain lies complete fulfillment and happiness while the pit of despair waits for me at the bottom.

With each step up the mountain, though, I get higher, feel happier, and feel lighter. But the ground is soft, so with each step up I slide back down a half-step. There never seems to be consistent progress forward. There is always something trying to pull me back down. But I keep walking, struggling, and fighting, and over time I make it higher and higher and higher. As I reach greater heights, I begin to realize how much more I am able to see now. I am able to stop, take a look around me, and everything is much clearer than it ever was before. I am able to look behind me and see just how far I've come.

As I look back, I can see places where I have slipped, maybe even fallen back. I can see other paths that would have been better to take to get where I am today. Regardless, with this new perspective, I have the opportunity to learn from my past so I can move forward better.

Fighting to rise against the slippery sands of life has made me stronger in many ways. The uphill climb has made my mental legs stronger. It has conditioned my mental lungs to be able to withstand longer and more difficult struggles. For example, the same struggle I may have once had at the bottom of the mountain now seems like nothing to overcome because of the strength I've gained.

There is a sense of accomplishment that comes with an acknowledgment of all the work and difficult steps taken so far. While I acknowledge I may never reach the top of the mountain, I have a sense of satisfaction when I look around me and see how far I've come.

In summary, as with so many topics in this book, I believe good men acknowledge difficult truths and fight evil, even when it lies inside themselves. *Especially* when it lies inside themselves, regardless of how difficult or insulting the truth may be to our egos. This is no different than with depression. Good men need to acknowledge the difficult truth of depression and then, in response, choose to make moral, rational, and common-sense decisions to heal. So, my encouragement to you is if you have reached the point where you believe you are struggling with depression, make a good decision today. Make the decision to get help, whether you work at helping yourself or seek help from someone else. Decide to take the first steps toward finding meaning, fulfillment and happiness.

How to fight depression:

The following is by no means an exhaustive approach to overcoming depression. It is meant to be a simple, straightforward framework for moving in the right direction towards healing.

1. Consult a physician.

   I understand this may be the last thing you want to do, but hear me out. Just like a bodybuilder who struggles to build muscle without protein in their body, a person can struggle to build happiness without dopamine, oxytocin, endorphins, serotonin, adrenaline, etc. in their body. Each of these chemicals plays a role in helping you with your sense of happiness. If you are fighting depression, it is likely your body struggles in one way or another with producing or using these chemicals. But how will you know you are deficient in them unless you see a physician who can find out? Think of it as the bodybuilder who struggles to build muscle deciding to visit a nutritionist. The nutritionist makes an assessment, finds out what the bodybuilder needs, and then prescribes the correct diet and/or supplements to help grow muscle. In the same way, seeing a doctor for depression will provide you with an assessment to help find out what happiness chemicals you have and/or lack. Or they may find out there is a problem with the systems in your body that produce and use these chemicals. The key is, by seeing a physician, you ensure you are covering as many potential causes as possible.

2. Exercise.

There are numerous studies that show exercise can be effective in reducing the symptoms of depression.[1,3,5,6,8] There are others that even find exercise to be as effective as medication[2-4] or psychological interventions[7] in the treatment of depression. But what kind of exercise should you do? How often? A systematic review (a review of multiple research articles on this topic) found exercise undertaken three times per week at moderate intensity, for a minimum of nine weeks, was the optimal amount of exercise to reduce the symptoms of depression.[9] Anecdotally, my mental state is always elevated when I exercise versus when I do not. As a practicing physical therapist, I have found many of my patients would report how much better their mood was, and how they felt in general, after exercising as well.

3. Recognize and acknowledge that life, and *all* the people in it, will never be exactly as you *expect.* All these things will, more often than not, fail to meet your expectations. The key is to accept the fact that disappointment *will* come, pain *will* come, and sadness *will* come. The key is to accept the inevitability of adversity, disappointment and sadness while at the same time understanding that each of these things is combatable. It may seem overly simplistic, but I like to flip expectations on their head. I try to "expect the worst and hope for the best." That way, I am living an existence where I am much more often pleasantly surprised than disappointed.
4. Use this three-step action plan each time something bad happens in your life. Repeat it each time you run into adversity. The first step: stop and *recognize* when something or someone hasn't gone your way. The second step: already know how you best deal with disappointment and *do that. Resolve* your issue as soon as possible. And the third step: *move on* with your life and with the people you care about. Recognize, resolve, advance. Recognize, resolve, advance. Recognize, resolve, advance.
5. *Release* past hurts. You can't hold on to the happiness available to you today if both hands have a death grip on all the hurts from yesterday. Let the hurts from your past go. As hard as it may seem, it *can* be as easy as forgiving and forgetting. It can be as easy as just letting the hurt go. At the end of the day, only you can allow the past to affect your present and future. *You* hold that power, no one else does. Use it!

CHPT. 12:
THE VOID

As odd as it may sound, sharing this concept with you may be the most exciting part of this book for me to write. It may not be the most important topic we've covered, but it's exciting for me to share nonetheless.

My excitement probably comes from the fact that I have learned so much from the time I spent in the void. Or it could be the deep gratitude I feel when I reflect on the positive changes in me, changes that occurred as a direct result of the time I spent in the biggest void of my life. Whatever it is, the concept of the void is exciting to share—especially if using it the way I did helps you as much as it did me.

While the void may be incredibly beneficial, it only remains so if you approach and use it correctly.

So, what is the void? "The void" I am referring to is the space in which you are alone. Alone physically, alone mentally, or both. It can be entered into voluntarily or you can be thrust into it violently for any number of reasons.

The void can take on many forms too. For example, it may be daily meditation—time you spend in deep thought or very little thought. The void could be taking a hike, being at the ocean, being in your backyard or in prayer. It can be wherever you are able to mentally access yourself. The void is somewhere, or some state, where you can both access and process your mental activity without distraction. On a larger scale, it can be part of, or within, a life circumstance. Circumstances such as being single, being unemployed, losing a parent or mentor who's always been your life's guide. It can be any mental or physical space where there is nothing but you and your thoughts. A void, yes. But a space of opportunity.

For me, the void was both on a large and small scale. On a large scale, after my divorce, I was single, had very few friends and not much contact with family. On a smaller scale, I had countless moments to sit in quiet places, spaces, and think.

During my void—which still purposefully exists in smaller scales and to varying degrees—I grew exponentially. Many quiet, lonely moments allowed me to assess myself. It allowed me to assess my life. It allowed me to ask myself tough and important questions. Questions like, what is my purpose? Where am I going? What should I be doing in the short and long-term? What mistakes did I make in the past? How can I avoid those mistakes in the future? How can I be a better dad? If I have the opportunity, how can I be a better husband? How can I help others not make the same mistakes I did? By acknowledging the void I was in and maximizing my time spent in it, I was able to answer these questions. But it took effort, patience, and honesty. It took work to be present in the moment and take the time to think self-critically. It took authenticity to accurately assess my past, my present, and where I needed to go in the future.

Assess Your Life

Maybe the biggest key to using the void for its maximum benefit is to assess your life first. Use the time and opportunities in the void to take a *deep dive* into your life. Assess where you are physically, mentally, and emotionally. Assess where you've been in those areas in the past, where you are now, and where you would like to be in the future. Assess what is good or bad about you in each area. Take detailed notes if you have to. Then you can make a plan. You can make a plan to bring about positive change for your future. For example, during the early part of my largest void I targeted insecurity as a major problem I needed to deal with. I wrote down detailed notes in all the areas I felt insecure. I wrote down specific circumstances, behaviors, and aspects of relationships in my past that made me feel insecure. I wrote down why I felt insecure in each situation and then began to research how to overcome insecurity. Once I had the tools to overcome insecurity, I began to use them to repair it in me. I was able to look at past situations and see where I had gone wrong. I could see where I made mistakes and how I could have thought and behaved differently. Through the process, I became aware of the root causes and triggers of my insecurity. Once I became aware of all these things, thought about all these things, I was able to leave insecurity behind me.

Personal Development

Insecurity was just one of the many areas I needed to improve and grow. Whatever the problem was, I knew I could only resolve it if I understood it and knew how to fix it. In order to continue to work on myself I read, I read, and then I read some more. I was determined to correct the problems within me. I was determined to make my present and future days brighter. I was determined to answer questions I needed the answers to in order to be a better man. Answers to the questions I noted earlier, but even to one of my biggest questions I didn't mention, such as is the God of the Bible real? Are the Bible's claims true? What is the proof they are true? Regardless, I had a lot of work to do. A lot of learning to do. A lot of learning to sort out my thoughts, my purpose, and life as a whole. So, I read and listened to people much wiser than me and learned.

My suspicion is you have a lot of learning to do as well. Maybe a lot less than I did, but I'm sure you have room to grow. And if we are being honest, we will never stop having room to grow. My hope is by reading this, you will take the opportunities in your void(s) to learn and grow, *now*. Especially if it prevents the rug of life from being ripped out from beneath you. Because before you know it, your life could be in free fall. In the blink of an eye, you could find yourself falling in a huge void, grasping at anything that might stop your fall. Anything to help you get a grip on reality.

If you happen to be reading this in the midst of your fall, my hope is this book will be something to grab on to. Something to stop your fall, get your bearings, and move forward in a positive direction.

The Void for Couples

Having relational troubles? Struggling in your marriage or feeling suffocated? Well, spending time in the void might help. This void specifically would be one in which you two purposefully spend some time apart with the commitment to grow and learn about each other during the process. This can take on many forms, but the basic idea is to commit, let's say, one specific hour a day to leave each other alone and do something productive for your relationship.

As for what to do specifically during this void, you could both read the same book on relationships. You can take the time to personally assess your life, your spouse's, and your family's. You can spend a good amount of time with a really good friend or mentor. Whatever you do, the goal should be personal and relational development. You should discuss what goals you each have with the other spouse and develop a framework for what you want to accomplish and how you each intend to accomplish it. If you can't come up with a plan, reach out to a marriage counselor, pastor, or book that can help.

For married couples, especially ones where it seems like one spouse is doing all the housework, caring for the children, etc., for example, I have a specific suggestion. And that is whoever does most, if not all, of the housework does not do any of that work for two to four weeks. There are specific rules though. First, the spouse taking over all the house care duties is not allowed to communicate in any way with the spouse who normally does them. No asking how to do laundry, food preparation, cleaning, etc. The spouse taking over the duties is on their own and they must make a *good-faith effort* to do a good job at them too. Second, the spouse taking over home care duties can only take the kids out to eat once per week. The spouse who is getting a break from the home care duties can and should go through how and when everything needs to get done before swapping roles but is no longer allowed to help afterward. The most difficult part might be for the spouse who usually does the work to sit back and let the other struggle, fail, and learn. The spouse taking over the home care duties should be left to figure all the nuances out, put in the work, and be committed to taking on the responsibility. The purpose of this is so the spouse taking over all the household duties will afterward have a much better appreciation of all the work it takes to do what the other has always done.

Now, two to four weeks may sound like a long time, but hear me out. Anyone can survive for a week. But for two, ideally four weeks, it is much more difficult. By the time four weeks comes along, the parent taking over the home care duties should have started to hit a bit of a groove with everything. Things that were really hard at first have now become part of the weekly or daily routine. Not only should the spouse who has taken over the home care duties have a *much* greater appreciation of all the work the other spouse has had to do, but they should have a number of added skills now to help out around the house moving forward. The two of you should then discuss who should be responsible for what house duties on a daily, weekly, and/or monthly basis.

A good man should be willing to humble himself and take on a challenge like this without question. And this is only one example of a way to do this. Overall, show your spouse you can and want to learn. Show your spouse you do and *will* help.

Purposeful Voids

Just as a couple can enter into a void on purpose, so can you enter any number of voids on purpose. And you should. Whether you set aside time to meditate, pray, read or just sit and think, you should purposefully enter into the void regularly.

For a religious person, entering a physical and mental space where there are no distractions can help you better discern your communication to and/or from God.

Whether a person is religious or non-religious, you can discern your own thoughts better by doing something like meditation. A mental place where you can process and project ideas better.

Similarly, reading a book can help you enter the void as well. When reading, you enter into a void that exists via a direct link between the information you are receiving and your brain and mind. While reading you are receiving information, oftentimes reflecting on it, and you begin to integrate that into your being, which allows you to grow personally.

Whatever the reason may be, and however you enter into a purposeful void, the process is very important. And the more regularly you do it the better. Make sure you take the time to unplug yourself from all that distracts people these days and learn from something you read or immerse yourself in your thoughts and see what changes happen.

CHPT. 13: CITIZENSHIP, SERVICE, AND LIFE BALANCE

Citizenship

Good men need to understand their nation's history. That remains true regardless of what country you live in. You need to know what is good about it and what is bad about it. You should also have a solid understanding of your nation's government and how it operates. You should keep up on current events, *from a variety of points of view,* too. The combination of these things will help you make informed decisions to shape your society for the better.

Not only can it help you make better decisions to help shape your society for the good, but it can help you better understand the role of government as a whole. It can help you understand that a good government should protect civilizations. It can help you understand that bad governments can destroy *any* civilization, even ones full of good people. Also, you can understand that unwise, good people can elect bad government officials. You can understand that good people can be fools. Good, ignorant people can unknowingly elect evil people into places of power. Good, ignorant people can be partly responsible for the destruction of a society. So, it is important to be knowledgeable when it comes to historical and current events.

Knowing the mistakes and benefits of past and current government *is critical* to helping shape current and future life for the better. Good men need to remember how government *should* function. They should always remember our communities' and individual rights are to be protected by our governments and not much more. They should remember our governments are there to protect us from threats to our freedoms. While many nations' governments do perform these duties, many do not. So it is up to good men to be able to see and understand the difference and work towards positive change.

For good men who do not live in free, honorable, or just nations, you should do your part to fight to change them. You should work to help you and your family live in a freer, more honorable, and more just nation. But again, this is very difficult to do without an accurate understanding of history.

In general, understanding your history gives you the best indicators for what works and what doesn't. It gives you clear indicators about what government should and should not do, now and in the future. This is just as true for nations and their governments as with anything else in life. Understand the history of where you live and where others live. Learn from the mistakes and successes of each. The combination of information will help you further good causes and help squash bad ones. Knowing what works and what doesn't will help you keep or bring about freedom. It can help maintain justice for all while preventing limited, or no, justice for all.

Service

I have talked a lot throughout this book about the need to be unselfish. Whether for your family or for your friends, I've talked at length about the need to be selfless. One area I have not talked about is in regards to community service. One could argue this may be just as important. If it isn't, it's a close second.

Serving others, especially people who you do not know personally, is vitally important. Serving others takes away nearly any selfish gain you could receive for helping a stranger. Selfless service is one of the most fulfilling things you can do. Of course, the whole idea of service is to help others, but it is important to note there are personal and meaningful benefits. More importantly, serving others helps raise up people in your community who are otherwise down. Serving others builds better communities without using many resources. Community service can even supplement or replace government intervention and dependence. Oftentimes, people even develop new relationships. They make positive new connections. In all, through serving others, people make life-changing decisions for others that help everyone rise. Decisions that elevate everyone involved and bring about much more joy.

Now, community service can take on many forms. It can look like serving your local homeless community, either with material resources or helping with operations at an existing homeless shelter. It can look like something as simple as picking up the trash in an underserved area of your community. On a larger scale, it can look like serving your entire country by joining the military. Whatever form your service takes, feeding into your community is very important. It brings people together. It shows there are still people left in the world willing to contribute something positive back into the world without asking anything in return.

Lastly, and maybe the most important way to perform community service, is to ensure you pass on your good values to the next generation. Ask yourself, what good is serving and living in a good society if it is just going to be destroyed by the next generation? Now, the good you do from serving today will last a short while, but all the work you do will eventually be wiped out by a generation behind you that doesn't hold the same values. Especially if they don't value the importance of good values, morals, and how to maintain a good society. Therefore, make sure you take the time to teach the next generation civics, history, and the difference between good and evil.

Balance

One of the most important lessons I have learned in life is to find balance. I have found this to be important in nearly all areas of life, with one exception. Morality. Why I exclude morality from balance is because a clear separation must be maintained between good and evil. You cannot balance good with evil and expect to achieve ultimate good. Evil will *always* taint the good you do. For anyone who understands anything about human nature, evil will eventually overcome good.

Think about a clear glass of water (good) and putting just a few drops of black dye (evil) into it. The water changes, becomes cloudy and looks nothing like it did before.

While morality is not an area to practice balance, there are countless other areas in life where balance *is* very important. The following are some key areas in life to practice balancing—some of which will be a review, but bears repeating.

Balancing between your personal needs and the needs of others

This may be the most difficult one to do on the list, but it is arguably the most important. Many times, in this book, I have focused on the good of being selfless. That doesn't mean there are not times, many times, when you need to take care of yourself first. For example, let's imagine *you* are the clear glass of water. If you are constantly pouring yourself out for others, eventually you become empty. Oftentimes, you become so thirsty as a result of your emptiness that you will do or use anything, or anyone, to fill yourself back up. In contrast, if you hold on to all the water you have, eventually it will get old. The water will get warm, gross, and eventually no one wants it. But when you have balance, you fill yourself first, pour some of yourself out and fill yourself back up again. You constantly balance between filling and pouring, filling and pouring, filling and pouring. You cycle through giving others your best while taking the time to fill and refresh yourself in-between.

Balancing between grace and fighting

It is very important to know when to fight and when to show grace. In a similar manner, knowing when to get angry and when to calm down. There is good anger, used to fuel a moral fight, and there is anger used for evil and immoral fights. Knowing the difference is key. So, learn how to balance between knowing when to pick up your sword to fight and when to lay it down. Run yourself through the mental checks to see if each situation is a moral fight worth having or not. Don't get sucked into doing evil by fighting a senseless or immoral battle.

Balancing your personal value with the need for personal growth

It is not easy to navigate life when you feel personally attacked all the time. That is why it is important to balance your personal value with your need for personal growth. You need to always remind yourself of your inherent value as a human being. With that settled, you can balance between attacks on your value and areas in which you *can* grow. Ideally, you get to the point where it is *very* difficult for anyone to make you feel less valuable. Very difficult for you to be offended. Then you can open yourself up to looking in the mirror and taking constructive criticism and/or being self-critical. *That's* when positive change and massive personal growth can occur because if you *feel* personally attacked all the time, you will always push back. You will rarely learn and rarely, if ever, grow. But when you have balance, you see the difference between the two and improve.

Balancing when to be strict and when to be soft with your kids

Want to grow and maintain a healthy relationship with your kid(s)? Then work hard to balance between when to let the little things go and when to put your foot down. As I have said before, you cannot lead an alienated heart and picking fights with your kids every chance you get will alienate them from you quickly. Be sure to nurture your relationship with your children. Learn to teach and guide them calmly and rationally as often as you can and use effective discipline. Learn ways you can make a very serious point, and take a very important stand, without poisoning the relationship. Know where the lines are that you do not want your kids to cross and find your balance right on each of those lines.

Balancing between providing and being present for your family

Good men want to provide for their families. Good men want to be there for them too. Ideally, good men do both. Finding a healthy balance between work and home is important. Learning to live within modest means so you can spend more time with your family may be a part of that. Some men don't have a choice though. Some men need to work a lot to provide enough. That's okay. It will just be more challenging for men in this position to be present for their family. If you are in this position, tackle the challenge head-on. Brainstorm ways to balance both. Step back. Assess your situation and find how you can best balance both.

Balancing between listening and talking

Knowing when to talk and when to listen is key to nearly every conversation you have. Some people want you to hear them while others want to listen to what you have to say. Regardless, the whole idea of having a conversation is to communicate something. Whether communicating an idea or feelings, the information shared is meant to achieve some goal. But how difficult is it to achieve that goal if the parties involved aren't on the same page? If the parties involved don't understand one another? This is why it is so important to balance listening with talking. You have to use your words, ears, and brain effectively to get things done. To really connect relationally with people, you need to balance well between the same. When in doubt, talk less, listen more.

Balancing between independence and dependence

Men typically approach independence and dependence differently depending on the circumstance. Take emotions, for instance. Most men prefer to handle their emotions independently. Whether in a healthy manner or not, most men prefer to handle emotions themselves. The problem comes when emotions have filled men to the point of overflowing and they act out. This is where balancing with more dependence than independence would be helpful. Whether you talk to a good friend, mentor, or your spouse, getting in the habit of talking about emotions is good. Men don't have to see this as taking the time to talk about their feelings but taking the time to talk about life. Usually, just discussing the struggles of life for men will release and relieve underlying emotions.

Now take physical needs, for instance. This is where men are usually much more dependent. Whether it be meals, some housework, laundry, etc., men usually rely on their spouse for these things. Some men are very independent in this area, but many more men are not. Regardless, my point is to become aware of areas where you should be more independent or more dependent. Take a look at the quality of your life and the lives of those around you. See how you can improve both with a better balance of independence and dependence.

CHPT. 14:

ADULT BOYS

Are you over the age of 21? Do you choose *not* to believe you have room to grow? Do you choose not to self-reflect or humbly listen to criticism? If so, this final chapter will likely be the toughest chapter for you to read. In fact, you probably won't get much out of it, assuming you read through it at all. If you are ready for some brutal honesty and can read the following with a deep sense of reflection and humility, this section could change your life; change it for the better and impact those around you positively as well.

Not all of this information will relate to you. In fact, none of this may relate to you, but for most adult guys I believe much of this will hit you right between the eyes. And it may hit you more than once. All I ask is you do your best to read it with an open mind, reflect on it, and respond to it in a positive way. Hopefully, your response results in you improving yourself. So just read, reflect, and respond. Read, reflect, respond. Read, reflect, respond.

Also, as you read, keep in mind the following rants are as much things I wish I could've told myself when I was younger as they may seem to be any criticism of you. Having been able to say some of these things to myself a long time ago, I may not have made such bad decisions and it may have helped me get my life on a better track. Ultimately, my hope is if these words do relate to you, they catch you at a point *before* you make the same, or worse, mistakes I did.

Get your act together!

To the adult boy, most likely still living in your parents' home: Seriously dude, get your act together! Are you really going to live in your parents' house forever? Are you *actually* going to make a real effort to get a job, move out of your parents' home and contribute in a meaningful way to your life? Are you going to make a meaningful effort to contribute to your family's lives and your community? Maybe you do have a job already, and if so, great! But if you are still at home and can honestly say to yourself you could be doing *a lot* more to be independent, why aren't you? Why aren't you taking control of your life and relieving your parents of a major burden (yes, you are that major burden).

Are you *really* (always) going to lean on Mom and Dad to bail you out of everything? Even if they are happy to do it, are you *always* going to expect them to assume responsibility for you? Are you always going to expect them to protect you from every difficult situation life *will* throw your way? Is that really what you want?

Maybe you should quit telling yourself and others you *will* do more *someday*. Maybe you should decide, *right now*, to get rid of your video games. To take inventory of your life and your purpose. Inventory what you find meaning in, what your skills are, what your strengths are, what your weaknesses are and come up with a first step toward pursuing a fulfilling and meaningful life.

In contrast to your current situation, imagine if, instead of draining your parents of energy, time and resources as a grown child, you were independent and feeding *into* your parents? What if you were an independent, hardworking man able to feed into them with your gratitude, your time (without expecting anything in return), and maybe even finances if needed (or not needed). Wouldn't providing a purpose-driven life be infinitely more fulfilling than a parasitic, neglectfully wasted one?

Now, to the adult boys who have a spouse and/or children. Even more so, you need to get your act together. Is your game console *really* more important than time spent with your spouse or family? Are the drugs and/or alcohol you consume more important than your spouse or family? How about your pornography consumption or any number of other addictions stealing the best of you from your family?

Do you really have to get together with your buddies multiple times a week or could you better balance between them and your family? What about your pride? Do you really have to win *every* argument? Are you *really* always right? Do you really have to revert back to your adolescent self and argue over things that just hurt the little boy inside you? Is it possible you may just need to grow up and mature? Is it possible you may simply need to realize you *need* to get rid of your video games, you *need* to control your addictions, you *need* to stop looking at porn, and you *need* to start self-reflecting and growing good character? The good news is, if you have read this book and have made it this far, I would say you're well on your way. While you may *need* this change, your spouse and family, arguably, may need it more. Remember, when you are better, everyone around you is better.

Turn off the TV and put your phone away

I'm not saying all the time, but a lot of the time. I get it, this isn't new news for most people. But whether I am repeating old news you've heard or bringing this up for the first time, we spend incredible amounts of time on our phones and/or being glued to a television screen. In the meantime, building relationships, building ourselves, and building those around us becomes less and less of a priority. That's *assuming* any of those things were a priority before you became consumed by screen time.

While watching a movie with your family, your spouse, or just your kids is pretty great, I want to challenge you to consider watching one instead of three. Engage with your family. Engage with yourself. Engage with the world, your hobbies, or community. Do something truly meaningful and do something that can have a positive impact on your tangible world. If you have to, set timers, limits, or schedules where you give yourself and/or your kids a certain amount of screen time. Go do something together or do something apart, but do something *meaningful, purposeful,* and *truly valuable.*

R-E-S-P-E-C-T

I have heard my whole life men just want respect from their spouse. Respect. Respect. Respect. I hear, "All I want is for my spouse to respect me. I just wish they would show me some respect."

I have heard my whole life that lack of respect from a man's spouse is the main source of relational struggles. Maybe that is true and maybe it isn't. Regardless, I have news for you guys—bad news for most—in regards to respect. *Respect is earned.* Respect is not a gift given freely. Respect is not given simply because it is demanded. Respect isn't given to you simply because you breathe. Authentic respect is *earned.*

You want *respect?* Be a good man. Put into practice the things we've discussed in this book and see if you don't get more respect. You may be respected more than you ever thought possible! Just remember, don't demand it. Don't expect it. Earn it.

Maturity

I am not talking about physical maturity but mental, emotional, and spiritual maturity. Discussing the importance of maturing in these areas is a perfect place to conclude this book. Why? Because becoming mentally, emotionally, and spiritually mature is the hallmark sign of a good man. It is the manifestation of taking the teachings of this book and living them out in your life.

For example, when you are humble, you show maturity. When you demonstrate moral and selfless behavior, you show maturity. When you make wise decisions, you show maturity. When you humbly learn the characteristics of a good man, internalize them and let them transform your outward behavior, you show maturity. Everything about being a good man is an indication you are a mature human being. Who doesn't like to be with or be around mature human beings?

All in all, I hope and pray you take this book and the words in it to heart. I believe becoming a mature, good man will transform your life. I believe moral standards, good behavior and a relationship with the God of the Bible can put you on such a higher level in life it is impossible to bring you down.

To be clear, God wants what is best for you and your life. And as weird as it may sound, not ever having met you, I want what is best for you and your life. Otherwise, I would never have written this book. I have no doubt there are people in and/or around your life who want what is best for you and your life as well too.

The real question is do *you* want what is best for your life? And if you do, how are you going to get it? I hope you see what I have laid out in this book is exactly how. But are you willing to humble yourself, learn, grow, and transform yourself into a good man? I sure hope so because I believe when you do, your slice of this world will be elevated. When hundreds, thousands, millions of good men elevate themselves and one another, true peace, love, and security will reign on this earth.

WORKS CITED

Fatherlessness

1. National Fatherhood Initiative. "Fatherless Children Statistics and Other Data on Fatherhood: NFI." *Father Involvement Programs for Organizations and Families*, www.fatherhood.org/fatherhood-data-statistics.

Depression

1. Antunes HK, Stella SG, Santos RF et al. Depression, anxiety and quality of life scores in seniors after an endurance exercise program. Rev Bras Psiquiatr 2005; 27(4):266–271.
2. Blumenthal JA, Babyak MA, Doraiswamy PM et al. Exercise and pharmaco- therapy in the treatment of major depressive disorder. *Psychosom Med* 2007; 69(7):587–596.
3. Blumenthal JA, Babyak MA, Moore KA et al. Effects of exercise training on older patients with major depression. *Arch Intern Med* 1999; 159(19):2349–2356.
4. Brenes GA, Williamson JD, Messier SP et al. Treatment of minor depression in older adults: a pilot study comparing sertraline and exercise. *Aging Ment Health* 2007; 11(1):61–68.
5. Chu IH, Buckworth J, Kirby TE et al. Effect of exercise intensity on depressive symptoms in women. *Ment Health Phys Act* 2009; 2(1):37–43.

6. Callaghan P, Khalil E, Morres I et al. Pragmatic randomized controlled trial of preferred intensity exercise in women living with depression. *BMC Public Health* 2011; 11:465.
7. Fremont J, Craighead L. Aerobic exercise and cognitive therapy in the treatment of dysphoric moods. *Cognit Ther Res* 1987; 11(2):241–251.
8. Singh NA, Clements KM, Singh MA. The efficacy of exercise as a long-term antide-pressant in elderly subjects: a randomized, controlled trial. *J Gerontol A: Biol Sci Med Sci* 2001; 56(8):M497–M504.
9. Stanton R, Reaburn P. Exercise and the treatment of depression: a review of the exercise program variables. *J Sci Med Sport.* 2014;17(2):177-182. doi:10.1016/j.jsams.2013.03.010
10. *What Is Depression?*, www.psychiatry.org/patients-families/depression/what-is-depression.
11. "WISQARS Leading Causes of Death Reports." *Centers for Disease Control and Prevention*, Centers for Disease Control and Prevention, webappa.cdc.gov/sasweb/ncipc/leadcause.html.

Pornography

1. "How Is the Porn Industry Worth Billions of Dollars?" *Fight the New Drug*, 9 Mar. 2019, fightthenewdrug.org/how-free-porn-industry-growing-in-fast-paced-digitized/.
2. Kuhn, S. and Gallinat, J. (2014) "Brain Structure and Functional Connectivity Associated With Pornography Consumption: The Brain on Porn." JAMA Psychiatry.
3. Malcolm, M. & Naufal, G. (2014) "Are Pornography and Marriage Substitutes for Young Men?" *Institute for the Study of Labor.*

4. "Pornography." *Enough Is Enough*, enough.org/stats_porn_industry.
5. Sabina, C., Wolak, J., Finkelhor, D. The nature and dynamics of internet pornography exposure for youth. (2008) Cyberpsychology and Behavior, 11 (6), pp. 691-693.
6. Simone Kühn, Jürgen Gallinat, "Brain Structure and Functional Connectivity Associated With Pornography Consumption: The Brain on Porn," JAMA Psychiatry 71 (July 2014): 827-834.
7. Sun. A., Bridges, A., Johnson, J. & Ezzell, M. (2014) "Pornography and the Male Sexual Script: An Analysis of Consumption and Sexual Relations." *Archives of Sexual Behavior.*
8. "The Effects of Pornography on Individuals, Marriage, Family, and Community," by Patrick F. Fagan, Ph.D., psychologist, and former Deputy Assistant Health and Human Services Secretary.
9. Weiss, Robert. "The Prevalence of Porn." *Psych Central.com*, 28 Mar. 2019, blogs.psychcentral.com/sex/2013/05/the-prevalence-of-porn/.
10. Wright, P., Tokunaga, R. & Bae, S. (2014) "More Than a Dalliance? Pornography Consumption and Extramarital Sex Attitudes Amoung Married U.S. Adults." *Psychology of Popular Media Culture.*

Human Sex Trafficking

1. "Global Estimates of Modern Slavery." *Ilo.org*, www.ilo.org/wcmsp5/groups/public/---dgreports/---dcomm/documents/publication/wcms_575479.pdf.
2. "The Link Between Pornography and Human Trafficking [2019]." *Ever Accountable*, 29 Oct. 2019, everaccountable.com/blog/the-link-between-pornography-and-human-trafficking/.

3. U.N. International Labor Organization: Profits and Poverty, The Economics of Forced Labor, 2014 - http://www.ilo.org/wcmsp5/groups/public/--- ed_norm/---declaration/documents/publication/wcms_243391.pdf

4. "What Is Human Trafficking?" *Department of Homeland Security*, 28 June 2019, www.dhs.gov/blue-campaign/what-human-trafficking.

STDs

1. "STD Facts - Chlamydia." *Centers for Disease Control and Prevention*, Centers for Disease Control and Prevention, 23 Jan. 2014, www.cdc.gov/std/chlamydia/stdfact-chlamydia.htm.

2. "STD Facts - Gonorrhea." *Centers for Disease Control and Prevention*, Centers for Disease Control and Prevention, 29 Jan. 2014, www.cdc.gov/std/gonorrhea/stdfact-gonorrhea.htm.

3. "STDs Continue to Rise in the U.S. Press Release." *Centers for Disease Control and Prevention*, Centers for Disease Control and Prevention, 8 Oct. 2019, www.cdc.gov/nchhstp/newsroom/2019/2018-STD-surveillance-report-press-release.html.

4. "Syphilis." *Mayo Clinic*, Mayo Foundation for Medical Education and Research, 19 Sept. 2019, www.mayoclinic.org/diseases-conditions/syphilis/symptoms-causes/syc-20351756.

Abortion

1. "Abortion." *Merriam-Webster*, Merriam-Webster, www.merriam-webster.com/dictionary/abortion.

2. "Data & Statistics - Reproductive Health." *Centers for Disease Control and Prevention*, Centers for Disease Control and

Prevention, 18 Nov. 2019, www.cdc.gov/reproductive-health/data_stats/index.htm.

3. "Fetus." *Merriam-Webster*, Merriam-Webster, www.merriam-webster.com/dictionary/fetus.
4. "Worldwide, an Estimated 25 Million Unsafe Abortions Occur Each Year." *World Health Organization*, World Health Organization, www.who.int/news-room/detail/28-09-2017-worldwide-an-estimated-25-million-unsafe-abortions-occur-each-year.

Meditative Masturbation

1. Department of Health & Human Services. "Masturbation." *Better Health Channel*, Department of Health & Human Services, 31 May 2015, www.betterhealth.vic.gov.au/health/healthyliving/masturbation.
2. Levine EC, Herbenick D, Martinez O, Fu TC, Dodge B. Open Relationships, Nonconsensual Nonmonogamy, and Monogamy Among U.S. Adults: Findings from the 2012 National Survey of Sexual Health and Behavior. *Arch Sex Behav.* 2018;47(5):1439-1450. doi:10.1007/s10508-018-1178-7
3. Rider, Jennifer R., et al. "Ejaculation Frequency and Risk of Prostate Cancer: Updated Results with an Additional Decade of Follow-Up." *European Urology*, Elsevier, 28 Mar. 2016, www.sciencedirect.com/science/article/abs/pii/S0302283816003778?via=ihub.

Made in the USA
Columbia, SC
05 July 2025

60344388R00078